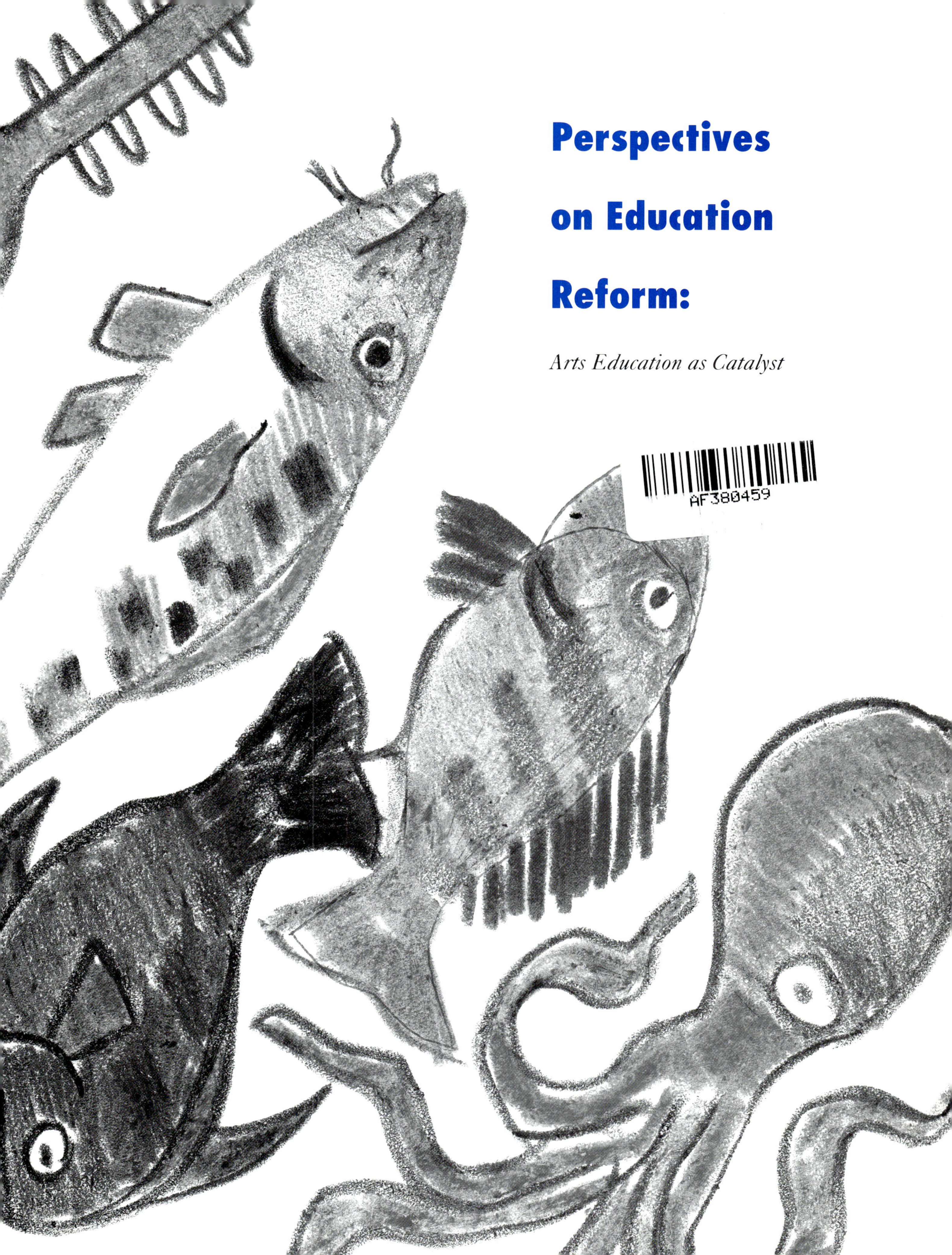

Perspectives
on Education
Reform:

Arts Education as Catalyst

AF380459

Getty Center for Education in the Arts
401 Wilshire Boulevard, Suite 950
Santa Monica, California 90401-1455

Library of Congress Cataloging-in-Publication Data
Perspectives on education reform : arts education as catalyst.
        p.   cm.
    ISBN 0-89236-296-0 : $5.00
    1. Arts—Study and teaching—United States.   2. Educational
change—United States.   I. Getty Center for Education in the Arts.
NX303.P49   1993
700'.7'073—dc20   93–32459
                                                          CIP

The illustrations that appear throughout
this publication were created by the Getty
Center's 1993 national conference participants, who drew with Crayola® products
provided courtesy of Binney & Smith, Inc.,
during the final conference session.

Table of Contents

Foreword...5

Perspectives on Education Reform

Education Reform in and through the Arts
GORDON M. AMBACH 8

Understanding Cultural Diversity through Arts Education
VADA E. BUTCHER 11

Equity and Access through Arts Education
MICHAEL GREENE...14

The Language of Technology Is the Language of the Arts
NANCY HECHINGER 17

The Challenge from Business to Arts Education
WILLIAM H. KOLBERG 20

The Challenge of Political Priorities to Arts Education
WILLIAM W. STATON 23

"Achieving National Education Reform: Arts Education as Catalyst"
San Francisco, California
February 4–6, 1993
Conference Summaries

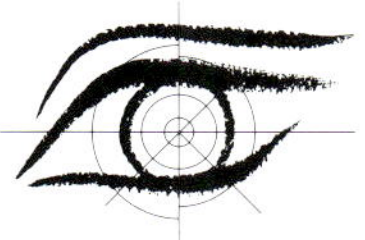

Conference Introduction..26

Keynote Address: Education Reform in and through the Arts 27

Strong Arts, Strong Schools...28

Challenges Facing Arts Education:
The Challenge from Business to Arts Education............................29
The Challenge from Education to Arts Education........................31
The Challenge of Political Priorities to Arts Education.................32

The Language of Technology Is the Language of the Arts..................34

Arts Education as a Catalyst to Reform:

    Interdisciplinary Learning 36

    Assessment 38

    Equity and Access 39

    Cultural Diversity 40

    Technology 42

Arts Education Partnership Working Group 43

Art Education's Value in Interdisciplinary Learning 44

Education Reform and Assessment in the Arts 46

Understanding Cultural Diversity through Arts Education 48

Equity and Access through Arts Education 49

Conference Summation 50

Final Words: Unity through the Arts 52

Postconference Session: Discussion of the Recommendations
of the Arts Education Partnership Working Group 53

Advisory Committee 54

Acknowledgments 55

As the debate about education reform in America continues to demand our attention, the answers to its more challenging questions are before our very eyes — in the arts. The arts hold a unique promise for educating our children in new ways. In fact, as we approach the new century, the engagement of children in learning and the future of education reform depend upon the arts and the fostering of the creative spirit.

As we stand on the threshold of the twenty-first century — marked by the convergence of diverse cultures, rapidly changing technologies, shifting economic relationships and rivalries, and the increasingly visual delivery of mass information — we need to see the future of arts education and general education as inextricably linked. Moreover, we need to continue to explore, document, and communicate this significant connection. If we are to be successful in revitalizing our educational system and sustaining arts education, we need to view the goals of education reform and the role of arts education in a fresh light.

In February 1993, the Getty Center for Education in the Arts convened its fourth national invitational conference, "Achieving National Education Reform: Arts Education as Catalyst."

This conference articulated a new vision for why we must, and how we can, place the arts at the center of learning in our nation's public schools. To quote our keynote speaker, Gordon M. Ambach, executive director of the Council of Chief State School Officers, "If the place of the arts is to be central to learning, we must ensure that the arts are at the heart of American education reform."

Over the course of the two-and-a-half-day conference, our speakers convincingly described the critical role of arts education in achieving the goals of education reform, particularly in the areas of interdisciplinary learning, multicultural education, assessment, educational technology, and access and equity. Because of the relevance of their messages, we felt it vital that those unable to attend hear their voices.

It is our hope that this publication, *Perspectives on Education Reform: Arts Education as Catalyst*, provides you with a greater understanding of the role of arts education in education reform. The following "perspective pieces" address the challenges confronting all of us who are committed to educating students. Taken together, they make a compelling case for arts education in contemporary education and illuminate the timeliness of its inclusion in reform efforts.

You will also find summaries of the presentations given by other national conference speakers.

These summaries contain the important ideas the speakers shared with the 1,500 attendees, including leaders and practitioners from the arts, education, business, politics, and technology. Our largest conference to date, "Achieving National Education Reform" marked a turning point for us in our efforts on behalf of arts education. It embraced the performing as well as the visual arts and provided a forum for a number of special events, including a public hearing on the National Assessment of Educational Progress (NAEP) in arts education planned for 1996 and a public discussion of the recommendations of the Arts Education Partnership Working Group. A summary of this latter session is also included in this publication.

We are pleased to present this publication, with its persuasive perspectives on how the arts can be a catalyst for achieving national education reform.

LEILANI LATTIN DUKE
Director
Getty Center for Education
in the Arts

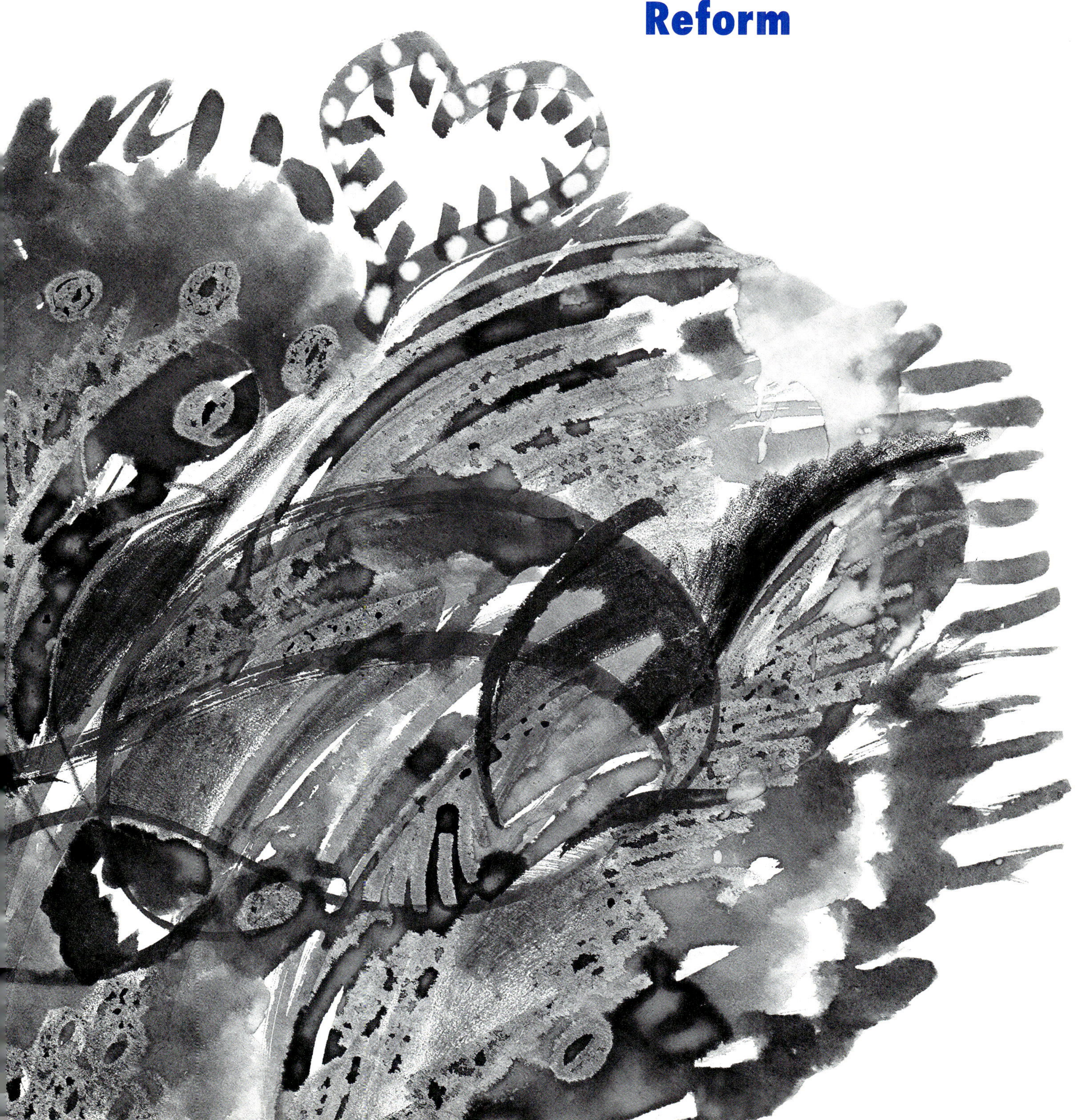

Perspectives
on Education
Reform

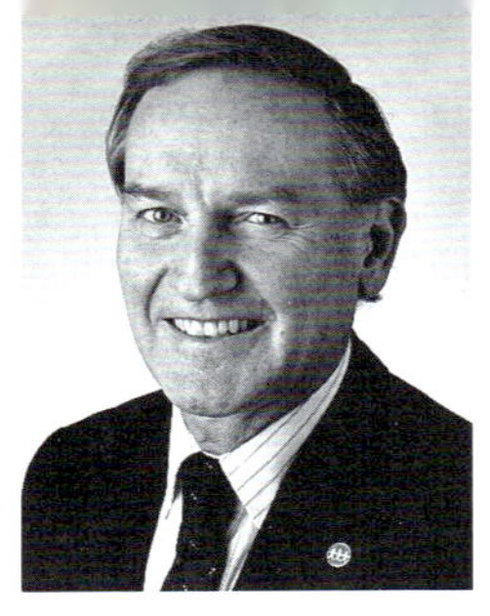

Education Reform in and through the Arts

GORDON M. AMBACH, *Executive Director, Council of Chief State School Officers*

In November 1992, American voters elected a new president, one who had conducted one of the most extraordinary campaigns in recent history. The credit for overcoming what seemed to be insurmountable odds and innumerable distractions was given to the campaign's strategist, James Carville. On the wall above Carville's desk was a sign that read, "The economy, stupid." It was a sign for Carville and his colleagues reminding them not to drift from the campaign's central message. As we advocate for education reform, we need a similar reminder to focus our message: "The arts, stupid." If the place of the arts is to be central to learning, then we must ensure that the arts are at the center of American education reform.

Given this prerequisite, there are five major areas of education reform in which the arts should figure prominently:

1. in establishing new goals for learning and creating standards as best practices;
2. in developing new assessments for measuring progress toward those goals;
3. in promoting higher-order learning through interdisciplinary studies and self-discipline;
4. in applying the wizardry of technology to learning, using imagery and sound to communicate as never before; and
5. in living the motto, *E pluribus unum*, "out of many comes one," celebrating both diversity and unity through the arts.

These five areas should be thought of as planks of a platform in the campaign for the arts in education reform.

Regarding the first plank, over the past five years there has been a remarkable, positive change in the American public's attitude toward the establishment of national goals and standards for education. Ten years ago, no one dreamed that we would ever have national education goals. Even five years ago, no one thought that the president and the governors could develop six national education goals. The place of the arts within these goals has been unclear; but, rather than focus on this ambiguity, we should simply declare that the arts are part of Goals 2000, the national education goals developed by the nation's governors and President Bush, and then behave accordingly.

As a result of the election and the change in administrations, some education policies will also change. But, the National Education Goals will remain; after all, President Clinton, the governor of Arkansas at the time the goals were written, was one of their principal architects. The president is expected to build his education programs around these national goals, and there are indications that the arts are included. For example, although Secretary of Education Richard W. Riley has not issued a formal statement on the arts, at his confirmation hearing, he said, "It would be my hope that, as the president-elect becomes a true leader in education, he and I would provide the leadership to let states and local school districts realize that arts in education is an absolute necessity. If, in this day and time, we do not tap into the creative side of a young person's brain in every possible way, then we are not going to have the innovation and the economic and cultural growth experience that this country must have."

But, the easy part is putting ideas such as these *in* the National Education Goals. The hard part is developing the objectives and the standards, and building the capacity in this nation so that, by the year 2000 and beyond, we can achieve them. The way in which we include or exclude a subject within our national expectations for education sends a powerful message that influences the media, government officials, and general discourse on what we value for our children and the country. How we engage the national education dialogue will determine whether the arts ride the wave of education reform or become submerged in its wake.

We must be clear that setting standards is not equivalent to setting minimum requirements. In business, the term *standard* means "best practice," and this is what we must ensure is understood with regard to the arts. Further, we must be prepared to renew our standards periodically. The debate surrounding standards and goals itself generates creativity and renewal, which leads to new objectives and practices. The standards in the arts that we are now struggling to develop will need to be revised continuously. Renewal and revision will keep the arts in the public debate and on the national agenda.

As Americans, we must begin to set our education standards in an international context. We have much to learn from other nations about their educational systems, particularly at a time when most American measures of educational assessment are being called into question. While international assessments of learning in geography, science, mathematics, and computers all have been conducted, there has yet to be an international assessment of learning in the arts. In developing new assessments for measuring progress toward these goals and standards, it is the arts educators, and those who assess the arts, who can take the lead. Portfolios and performance assessments in the arts are long-standing assessment models that can be used in other areas of learning.

Perhaps the most significant element of education reform to emerge in the past several years has been the focus on developing higher-order thinking skills in all children. The new industrial environment requires workers who can grasp complex material and organize their own work so that they are more productive. Students must learn to combine knowledge and process to be inventive and solve problems. Learning in and through the arts is an essential vehicle to this end. To develop higher-order thinking skills, students should be exposed to different disciplines and

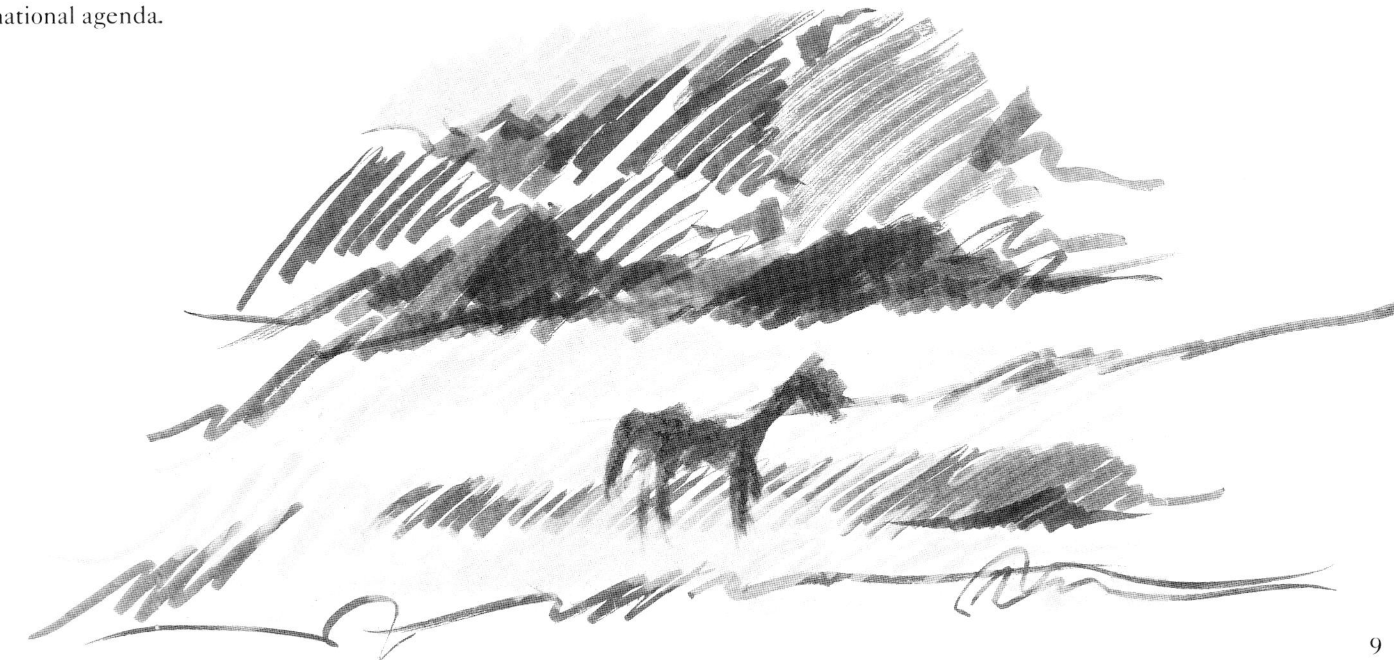

forms of study. Discipline-based arts education presents a combination of aesthetics, criticism, history, and production that develops students' capacities to integrate what is learned in each of these dimensions. The discipline-based approach connects the study of history, science, geography, literature, mathematics, and the arts. The concept of the discipline-based approach is a major force in the debate surrounding interdisciplinary studies in other fields. The reforms that are under way in the arts are central to changes in interdisciplinary pedagogy within the overall education reform movement.

Communication technologies are playing new and important roles in such areas as creating and conveying messages through art forms. Yet, in teaching students to communicate, the focus remains on reading, writing, speaking, and listening, rather than on *creating* and *interpreting* images, movement, sounds, and emotion. But, imagery is central to television and the other powerful communication technologies that have a special influence on young Americans. In education reform, the expansion of learning technologies in the schools must be related directly to increasing a student's capacity to understand and use images, sounds, and data in technological communication. In other words, learning in the arts is essential to the effective use of technology, which is in turn central to the capacity of modern communication.

The education reform movement is struggling to help students to understand the value of *E pluribus unum;* learning in the arts is central to that understanding. American students of diverse backgrounds need to know and cherish their own history, while at the same time sharing the common experiences that make us one people. The arts offer a most impressive means by which we may perpetuate and convey the diversity of our cultural roots. An understanding of African-American, Latino, Asian-American, and Native-American traditions is, for example, conveyed with unique impact through the arts. The arts unify and represent our commonality while celebrating our diversity.

As we recall great eras of accomplishment, we think of Egyptian pyramids, Baroque music, Greek sculpture, Aztec temples, Chinese ceramics, and African carvings, to name but a few. These accomplishments serve to communicate the dreams, beliefs, aspirations, and accomplishments of our ancestors. Our culture will be known and remembered by its arts. If we hope that our legacy will have the esteem of great ages past, we must place the arts at the center of our culture and at the center of our learning.

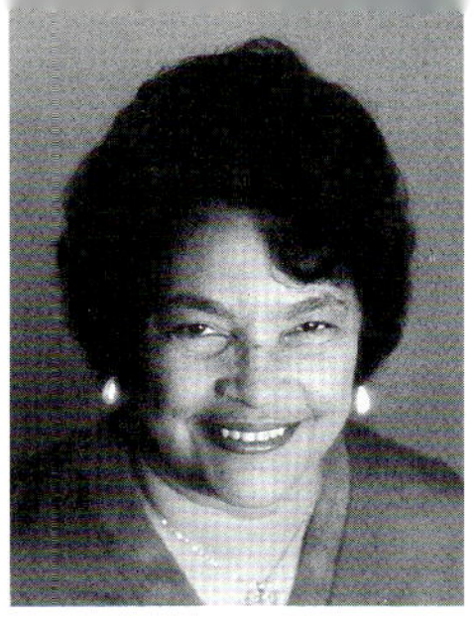

Understanding Cultural Diversity through Arts Education

VADA E. BUTCHER, *Dean Emerita, College of Fine Arts, Howard University*

One of the most challenging tasks facing the world today is that of forging mutual understanding and respect among ethnic enclaves. Currently, there exist conflicts between tribes in Nigeria, between Muslims and Hindus in India, and between Serbs, Bosnians, and Croats in what used to be Yugoslavia — which has escalated into brutal warfare and the horror of "ethnic cleansing." Such conflicts may result from long-standing feuds, from the need to assert ethnic identity after generations of repression, or from successive waves of immigration and aggression that often occur in the never-ending competition for a better quality of life. When we look at the cultural climate in the United States in terms of its ethnically mixed society, we discover something of a microcosm of much of the strife that is confronting the world.

Over a 500-year-period, the population of the United States was built from a mixture of indigenous groups and people coming primarily from Western Europe, West Africa, Mexico, and Asia. Although founded on the principles of social equality, for most of its history, the country has been dominated by the European ethos. Only since the middle of the twentieth century has this dominance been challenged by other sectors of the population, including African Americans, Chicanos, and Native Americans. Other previously ignored sectors of society such as the aged, women, and the physically challenged, have joined in the demand for equity. These demands cannot be ignored.

The most recent demographic studies indicate that there are more adult females than there are adult males; and that by the year 2000, senior citizens will outnumber those under the age of eighteen; and that by the middle of the twenty-first century, so-called minorities will make up the greater portion of our urban population. If we are to avoid the kind of social unrest faced by so much of the world today, then we must ensure that our public education system provides learning experiences that will prepare students to live comfortably and productively among those whose worldview is different from their own. Curricula can no longer be limited to that of the Greco-Roman tradition, with only passing references to other civilizations. Instead, there must be acknowledgment of the validity of other cultures and other concepts of knowledge. The public education enterprise must be structured as dialogues between ethnic groups that are equally concerned with the common good of humankind. Studies of cultural diversity should be modeled after the processes of intellectual diversity. This approach will reveal the common concerns of all the peoples of the world and the basic similarities of all citizens of the United States. By approaching education in this way, our society will avoid the dangers of being divided into competitive ethnic compartments.

Although some have voiced valid concerns that attention to issues of ethnic diversity might dilute the quality of the curriculum and lead to superficial study, this need not be the case. Courses in ethnic studies should not be merely the simple accumulation of facts, but the expansion of cultural horizons through critical engagement of different points of view. Standards of excellence can be ensured by requiring students to engage in serious comparative scholarship, the intellectual analysis of cultural phenomena, and the use of the finest products of human intellect and imagination as exemplars. Equity need not preclude excellence. On the contrary, no educational enterprise that ignores the history, the highest thought, and the creativity of a sizable segment of the national population can be *truly* excellent.

But the hard truth is that, despite the diversity and excellence of a curriculum, television and other media have become mass educators, often contradicting what is taught in schools. For example, a young Indian boy who has watched six hours of "cowboys and Indians" on television may very well question just what kinds of opportunities are truly available to him. To leave these images of the popular entertainment media unanswered is to risk creating fragmented and isolated population sectors. A most effective way of increasing the impact of what is taught in schools and counteracting negative images in the media is through arts education. Students should be exposed to the intellectual and physical demands of aesthetic study. They should be aware of the differences between art and entertainment and the role of art as a reflection of human existence. The arts play a unique role in documenting the psychological and emotional trauma suffered by all minorities as they attempt to shape their worldview to accommodate that of the dominant culture. Faced with the necessity of preserving a sense of self-worth while often coping with an alien language, manners, and codes of conduct, minorities cultivate a kind of multiple identity. Pan-African activist W. E. B. DuBois called this a "double consciousness," that is, the sense of always looking at oneself through the eyes of others. References to this uneasy dualism, which permeates every facet of minority life, are numerous in the literary, visual, and performing arts.

Minorities also share an enervating and sometimes terrifying sense of isolation from mainstream society, which often causes them to question the reality of their existence. It is no accident that African-American artists frequently use their work to describe themselves as invisible and without consequence in the world. But herein lies the most compelling case for the study of ethnic arts education. Imagine the insight and understanding such ethnic arts study brings to a student's own sense of self as well as others' understanding of that student.

The cultivation of literacy in the arts may actually preserve life itself by promoting understanding among ethnic groups whose daily existence seems to be on the precarious edges of violent confrontation. To be successful, arts education courses reflecting the unique characteristics of our society must, at the very outset, recognize the complexity of our cultural diversity — what James Lynch describes as the "pluralisms within our pluralism." For instance, although native West Africans and their descendants coalesced long ago in their struggle against slavery, the 371 Native-American tribes still existing in this nation today continue to maintain cultural distinctions despite intertribal borrowing and the recent pan-Indian movement. The term *Hispanic* is distressingly inadequate in identifying our Spanish-speaking population, which includes Americans of unmixed Spanish descent, stateside and island Puerto Ricans, Cubans, and Chicanos, who themselves differentiate between Texas, New Mexico, and California groups. The recent and continuing arrival of Asian immigrants not only increases the intricacy of our pluralism but predicts the fluidity of our ethnic profile for years to come.

Our demographic diversity is equaled only by the complexity of the arts as academic disciplines and as documentation of cultural history.

Students should be made aware of the importance of indigenous folk art, urban folk art, media art, and fine art as reflections of human existence. And every arts education course should emphasize the necessity of applying appropriate criteria to the evaluation of the arts of ethnic cultures. For example, Puerto Rican *plenas*, Tejano *corridos*, Kiowa peyote songs, and African-American blues each have their own standards of excellence, and the performances of these genres cannot be judged by common criteria.

The skill of understanding art as a reflection of culture can begin early in a student's education. For instance, the mastery of West African polyrhythms, the performance of Puerto Rican game songs, and the fabrication of Hopi kachina dolls are well within the grasp of elementary school students, who can easily understand both the structure of these works and their functions in society. At the secondary school level, the production of artworks that reflect our nation's cultural diversity should be the culmination of critical analysis and intellectual exploration of their role in the societies they represent. For example, it is possible to trace the complete history of Blacks in the United States through their music, and a comparable study of the arts of other ethnic groups can be equally rewarding. Indeed, some milestones of our cultural history may be completely understood *only* through the legacies of our artists. The Chicano murals that adorn the exterior walls of many of our urban structures, the desperate Native-American ghost dance, and the bittersweet musings of the Harlem Renaissance poets are examples of these legacies. Students who are taught to see, hear, and understand the wondrous cultural works of their own and other ethnic groups cannot help but rejoice in the good fortune that has made them a part of this marvelous tapestry called the United States of America.

With so much at stake, teachers of the arts are indeed indispensable and crucial as a part of education reform. Educators must seek increased support for ethnic arts study from their communities. Vigorous championship of ethnic arts education should be taken to the various policy and decision makers, ranging from boards of education and university trustees to legislators and foundations that influence public education by the disciplines they choose to fund. The message is clear. There is only so much the sciences can tell us about cultural diversity in the United States. While they can measure economic impact and population trends, only the arts can reveal the spirit and soul of a nation committed to social equity. Only the arts can celebrate the nation's triumphs and mourn its failures in pursuit of this ideal. And only the arts can interpret its dreams for the future unity of its peoples.

Students who are taught to see, hear, and understand the wondrous cultural works of their own and other ethnic groups cannot help but rejoice in the good fortune that has made them a part of this marvelous tapestry called the United States of America.

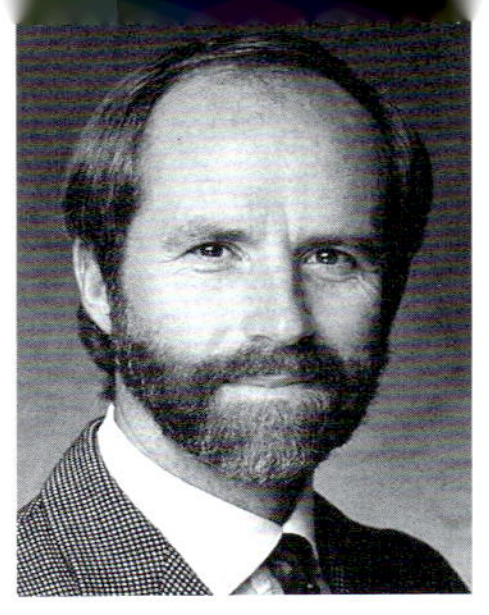

Equity and Access through Arts Education

MICHAEL GREENE, *President and Chief Executive Officer, National Association of Recording Arts and Sciences, Inc.*

If we are to stop the erosion that has decimated arts education in this country, we must effectively articulate the role that the arts play in addressing questions of diversity, access, and equity. In recent years, the professional and media discourse surrounding the nation's educational system has reinforced the idea of two competing ideological viewpoints. These two camps are represented, most typically, as

1. the back-to-basics conservatives who pray to the gods of math, science, and Eurocentricity and
2. the dark nemesis of free-thinking radicals who are hell-bent on trashing the canons and rule books in order to make room for multiculturalism and self-expression.

While the debate will continue to generate lengthy tracts for years to come, this "either or" approach is in fact a false dichotomy. It is the result of an outmoded worldview in which everything is reduced to black or white.

This "black or white" mentality must be replaced with an inclusive educational agenda that engages both sides of a person's brain and sacrifices neither discipline nor personal expression. We must codify new canons that play to the strengths of our heterogeneous society. We must redeploy our nation's resources in a way that ensures our cultural survival. We must break down these principles into tasks that each community and each school system can implement.

At the National Academy of Recording Arts and Sciences, through such vehicles as the televised Grammy Awards, we are calling attention to these issues. A major part of what the Academy does centers around monitoring the cultural environment for music and art in this country. And it has become clear that there are major challenges and opportunities facing music and art and the educational community in general.

For too many children in the nation's school system, the opportunity to learn about America's rich musical heritage and participate in school music programs has been severed — casualties in a war of narrow mind-sets and misappropriated resources. This has been caused by an erosion of America's cultural values. In its rush to catch up with other countries, the United States has squandered the very qualities that helped to set this country apart from all other countries in terms of artistic innovation. There is a good reason why such companies as Sony, Philips, Bertelsmann, and Matsushita spend billions of dollars buying this nation's record companies and archives. They realize that Americans are the supreme creators and purveyors of art as it relates to media.

One of the most important ways in which to enthuse children about music is to help them both intellectually and emotionally gain access to and reconnect with the music of this nation and the music of their own cultural groups. In the summer of 1992, after the Los

In its rush to catch up with other countries, the United States has squandered the very qualities that helped to set this country apart from all other countries in terms of artistic innovation.

Angeles disturbances, a youth summit involving some 1,200 of the area's youngsters was convened. So often, what was heard during this summit were children describing a slow but steady reduction of arts in their school programs until all arts programs in South Central Los Angeles had disappeared entirely. One girl described how her music class had been the one place she could regain her identity and find strength. The elimination of the music class eliminated her emotional context for success. Soon afterward, she dropped out of school.

Cutting arts programs out of a curriculum is tantamount to shutting off the access to these children's identity. Such actions remove the humanity from a child's education. Singer/songwriter Roseanne Cash has described a similar experience in her schooling. As a student, she was allowed almost no room for personal expression. She said that her artistic side was not valued or validated by her educators, and she spent her formative years feeling like a freak of nature.

It has been estimated that nationwide, during 1993, more than 300,000 children will drop out of school. We are facing a profound crisis. Innovative ways of keeping these students engaged must be developed. Some schools have begun to turn the tide on falling grades and dropouts by again requiring arts and music curricula. For instance, one of the poorest schools in the South Bronx is Saint Augustine's, a Catholic school. In 1985, it faced the prospect of closing due to low enrollment. To increase enrollment and student interest levels, the school administration made art and music a central part of the curriculum. Enrollment tripled, and reading and math scores improved by 28 percent. The improvement shown by these students is mirrored throughout the country, whether they be in remote rural settings or stark urban environments. Wherever music and art are a mandated part of the curriculum, students engage in *all* their classwork at higher levels.

By imagining music and art as isolated from or superfluous to the "traditional" core courses, we deny children the tools that they *need* to have. It is no accident that the countries succeeding in preparing their students for the twenty-first century already recognize music and art as vital means of teaching fundamental skills. It took more than fifteen years to undermine arts education in this country — and we're not going to remedy it in two or three years.

Ernest Boyer of the Carnegie Foundation said:

The arts are an essential part of human experience; they are not a frill. We recommend that all students study the arts to discover how human beings communicate, not only with words but through music, dance, and the visual arts. Now, more than ever, all people need to

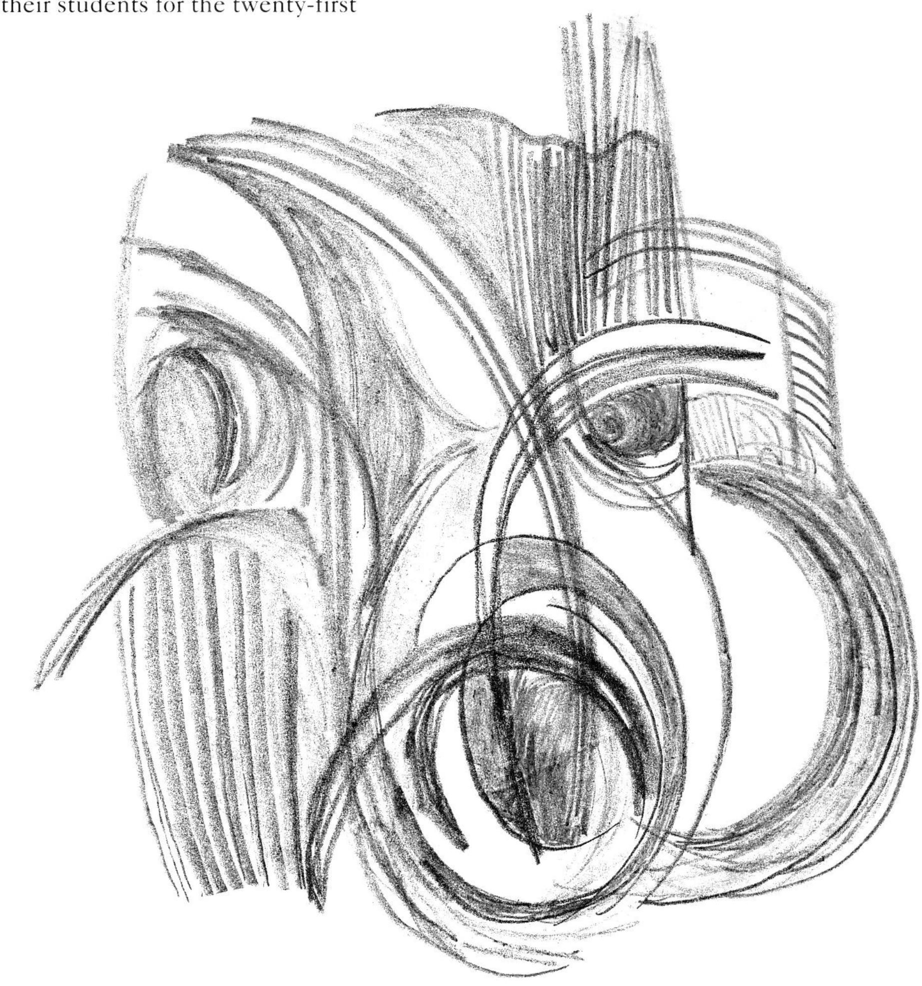

We are faced with some potential outcomes about which we must ask, "What then of civility and joy?" We could refuse to recognize that the arts are basic to what it means to be an educated human being. We could keep the arts as the pet sacrificial lamb of the educational budget. Fewer and fewer of our children would receive an education in the arts, and they would not learn how to listen to music or understand visual arts. The viselike pressures on the educational dollar might continue their squeeze. What then? Only the school districts having the biggest tax bases will survive. Only those having an entrenched arts program will continue to grow. Only the school boards, superintendents, and principals who *already* care will ensure that civility and joy are passed to our children.

If present trends continue, music and art will become a privilege tied to family and class economics — the beginnings of a cultural caste system. Music and art will no longer be cultural treasures of the country or in any of the states. Music and art will cease to unify but instead will divide. Instead of a tool for self-discovery, art will become a source of alienation.

Today, music and art education are increasingly being made available only to the privileged. In our inner cities, where low tax bases and massive education cutbacks have left educational institutions in shambles, children know nothing of their musical heritage. They know nothing of their history, their roots. They have no sense of pride about the fact that jazz music, rock and roll, African music, folk music, and blues music are all part of their collective culture.

As we address these questions, it is essential that we avoid getting bogged down in the old dichotomies. We must continue to emphasize the importance of cultural diversity, teach improvisational skills along with sight reading, and empower individual teachers to employ innovative instructional techniques. We are at a crossroads, and we have the opportunity to change. If, over the next six months, we reach any lower than the highest-possible plateau, we are making a big mistake. A strong, unified voice is required to convince the Clinton administration to set the tone, making arts and music prerequisites for high school graduation.

Together, and only together, will we see the arts restored to their proper place in America's educational system. The time has come to set aside personal and political differences. We must chart the future for our children by giving them a comprehensive, multifaceted arts education. The arts will ensure the vitality of our educational system and our culture. We can accept nothing less.

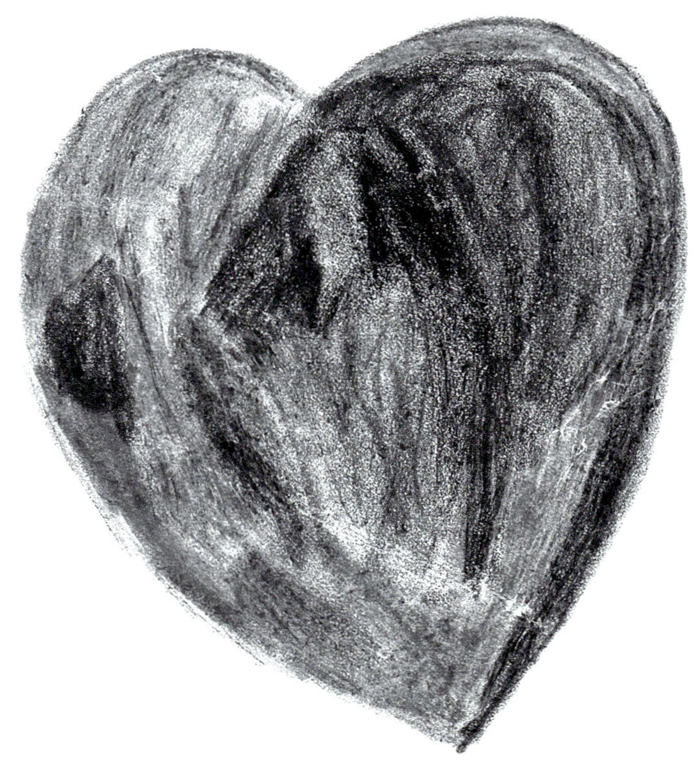

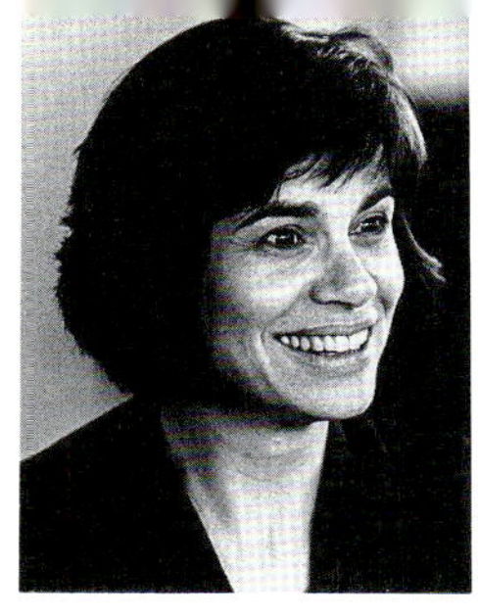

The Language of Technology Is the Language of the Arts

NANCY HECHINGER, *Founding Partner, The Edison Project*

In describing art, there are certain words that immediately come to mind — for instance, *creativity, imagination, invention, inspiration,* and *personal expression.* Art also evokes something ineffable, something that triggers a physical effect because it is so right or, sometimes, because it is so wrong. None of these are words that one would use to describe technology. But, the promise of technology is the unleashing of a new and rich form of expression.

The Edison Project (see page 18) has combined the essence of art and the promise of technology to design and build a national system of private schools. A fundamental idea behind the Edison Project is to step outside of the infrastructure, in which there are rules, regulations, and traditions, and explore what would happen if one began with a clean slate.

The Edison schools will bring electronic technology to every aspect of the system. This infusion is intended to change every aspect of school life profoundly. How children learn and how teachers teach, as well as how schools communicate with parents, will be improved with technological advances. Further, the assessment of student and teacher work and the overall system operation will be enhanced by these new technologies. The Edison Project sees technology as a tool for building on natural human curiosity, unleashing creativity and exploration. Truly dazzling technology is invisible, easy to use, and an enrichment and enhancement to both teacher and student.

The schools will be networked so that children in different regions can work together. Curriculum materials will be flexible and responsive to teachers' needs. The Project will have electronic libraries, multimedia offerings, and video documentaries. The Edison Project recognizes that technology does not make a good school; rather, it is the teachers, the curriculum, and the human interaction of families and educators. But technology in the hands of a great teacher can help to make a great school.

Computer technology and interactive media rely on the language of the arts — images, sounds, colors, and movements — to engage children in new ways of learning about the arts and other subjects. Both art and technology are central to the Edison Project's design. Art is a part of the core curriculum, both in practice and appreciation. For instance, every child will learn to play a musical instrument, students will sing together, and they will learn music history. All children will have visual art and music classes five times a week, as often as they will study mathematics. The curriculum has been so designed because there are several studies that suggest a significant correlation between children who study music and high SAT scores. There is also evidence of a correlation, albeit less strong, between the visual arts and higher test scores. That is why charcoal, crayons, clay, *and computers* will be available in the classroom to all the students and teachers as well as to the community.

More important than test scores is the fact that the arts inspire and compel, which is what every teacher wants — a fertile ground for student-based exploration.

The Edison Project does not consider art as just a separate subject. Instead, it is woven throughout the curricula. Art serves as a primary motivator, a subject in which the learner sets the agenda. More important than test scores is the fact that the arts inspire and compel, which is what every teacher wants — a fertile ground for student-based exploration. A key instructional method in the Edison Project curricula is project-based experiences, which allow for greater multidisciplinary study. Teachers and students are encouraged to employ their creativity.

The ineffable aspect of art also is central to the Edison Project design. This quality can be found in lessons, from which some of the world's finest art began. A great lesson is focused, clear, distilled, and even elegant — it has the essence of truth. And it is interesting. For instance, think of Paul Klee's *Pedagogical Sketchbook*, think of most of the religious art of the ages, think of music — Bach wrote *The Well-Tempered Clavier* for his six-year-old to break up the tedium of playing scales! Yet, it is arguably one of the greatest pieces of music ever produced. Wouldn't it be wonderful if instructors paid as much attention to instruction in math, in science, and in history? The Edison Project thinks so. The intention of the team is to create a "well-tempered" curriculum that aspires toward art. Teachers will be encouraged to think of themselves as coaches, guides, maestros, and mentors.

The torch is being passed to a new generation of educational technologists. But we are at a crossroads. One road will let us continue to employ technology in a linear, formulaic fashion, for drill and practice. If we take the other road, we begin to think in terms of art and creative expression — how people learn, what people enjoy doing. We think of words like *exploration* and *curiosity*, *resources*, and *open-ended*. The tools are available, but to develop truly great electronic resources and applications we need artistry, creativity, genius, and people who are as passionate about education as they are about technology.

Someone said that a nation at risk ought to take some risks, and the Edison Project is a risky proposition. The downside to this risk is fairly obvious; but, the upside is the offer of limitless possibilities for our children and our world.

Technology is just a means — a marvelous tool — and it is time to begin using it toward some marvelous ends: art and education. The three are inseparable.

About the Edison Project

The Edison Project has emerged as one of the many responses to education reform in the early 1990s. The mission of the Edison Project is to demonstrate that a high-quality education can be offered at a reasonable price to a cross-section of children. This private school system is intended to operate at the same cost per pupil as public schools.

As of mid-1993, the first fifty Edison schools are scheduled to open in 1996. By early in the twenty-first century, the Edison Project plans to have 1,000 schools across the country in its system. The Project's design is being created by

a seven-member core team headed by Benno Schmidt, the former president of Yale University. Currently, the team is working on a conceptual design for the program. As the team stepped outside the traditional educational infrastructure, it began by asking the most basic of questions, such as: Is a classroom needed? Is a place called school needed? What's wrong with spelling bees?

In trying to answer these questions, the team visited schools around the country, interviewing teachers and researchers.

Among its discoveries, the team reports it found the country to be in a period of great reform verging on revolution. It encountered great schools and wonderful teachers;

however, no one was able to point to a truly great education system. Creating a great system is the goal of the Edison Project. The Project seeks to establish a system that serves students, teachers, and parents; provides resources; and encourages innovations without an unwieldy and stifling bureaucracy.

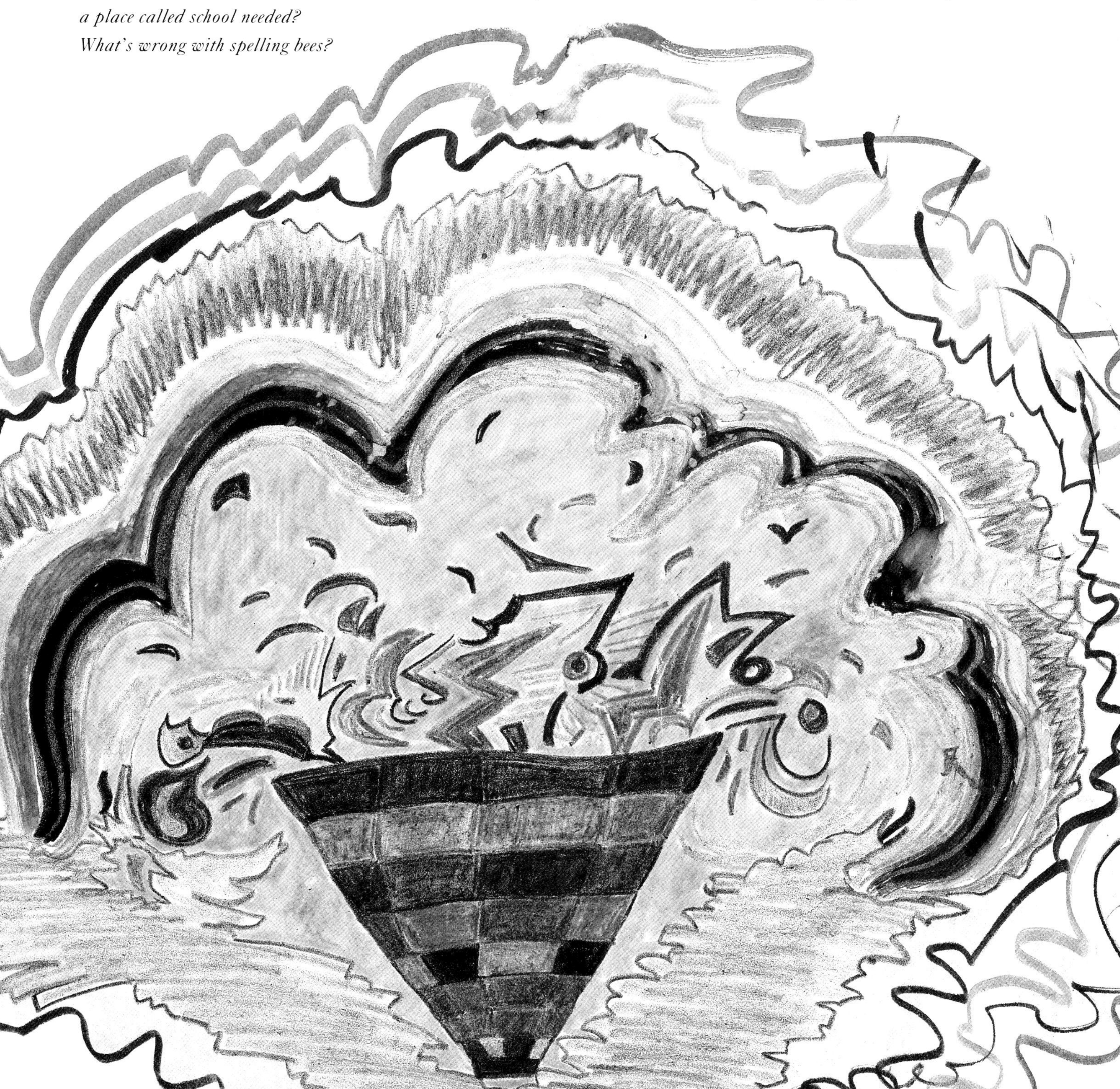

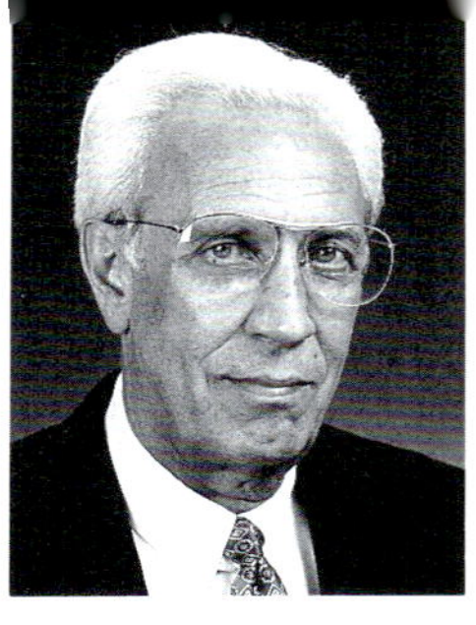

The Challenge from Business to Arts Education

WILLIAM H. KOLBERG, *President, National Alliance of Business*

As recently as a few years ago, no representative of a major national business organization would have felt comfortable confronting issues of education reform, let alone the role the arts play in achieving such reform. But the business world has changed immeasurably. Corporations are experiencing radical changes in the definition of work and in their needs for information, knowledge, and technology. Therefore, if businesses are going to have the types of workers needed to thrive in this changing environment, then the reform in public education must be equal to the change in business. Leading the charge in advocating necessary education reform is the National Alliance of Business.

American business is evolving. It can no longer rely on the mass production of goods and services or on a work force that may be functionally illiterate (reading at less than a seventh-grade level and performing arithmetic at less than a fifth-grade level). Today's global market and technological growth require every worker to solve problems, to work in teams, and to be creative. Now, more than ever before in our history, the success of U.S. business is dependent upon the quality and flexibility of the American work force. Business managers must be able to lead their workers into ever-higher levels of performance and productivity. Yet, with American businesses facing ever-increasing competition, the inability of the current educational system to turn out a world-class work force is well-known.

American students consistently rank last or near last in international comparisons measuring competency in math, science, and biology. Approximately 25 percent of all high school students drop out of school, and many having high school diplomas are functionally illiterate. Without additional investment of considerable time and money on the part of business, these people are virtually unemployable.

American business believes that a radical education reform strategy must begin now with a set of national standards and assessment systems and corresponding curriculum frameworks. These three elements, set at internationally competitive levels, need to be voluntary and adopted on a state-by-state basis. The United States is alone among industrialized Western countries in that it does not have national standards or assessments.

The American business community further believes that there are certain skills and abilities that *all* students need if they are to be successful in our society. Curriculum content should reflect high expectations for all students, even if it means employing varied methods of teaching students according to their individual learning styles.

A two-year study entitled "What Work Requires of Schools," undertaken by a commission appointed by the secretary of labor, defines what skills businesses require of entry-level workers. The findings serve as an introduction to the challenge business brings to arts education in seeking education reform. Three groups of skills were identified:

1. reading, writing, and mathematics;
2. creative thinking, decision making, and problem solving, including knowing how to reason and how to learn; and
3. personal qualities, such as a sense of responsibility, self-esteem, sociability, self-management, and honesty.

It is interesting to note that this foundation rests heavily upon skills that business has never before considered a part of the goals of education. The study also describes "five competencies" that all students must attain:

1. the ability to manage resources;
2. interpersonal skills, such as teamwork and leadership;
3. information acquisition and application skills;
4. system skills; and
5. technological skills.

Within the study, the importance of the three "foundation" skills and the five "competencies" is described as

. . . essential preparation for all students, both those going on directly to work and those going on to higher education. Thus, the foundation and the competencies should be taught and understood in an integrated fashion that reflects the workplace context in which they are applied. After examining the findings of the cognitive sciences, the most effective way of learning skills is in context, placing learning objectives within a real environment rather than insisting that students first learn in the abstract what they will be expected to apply.

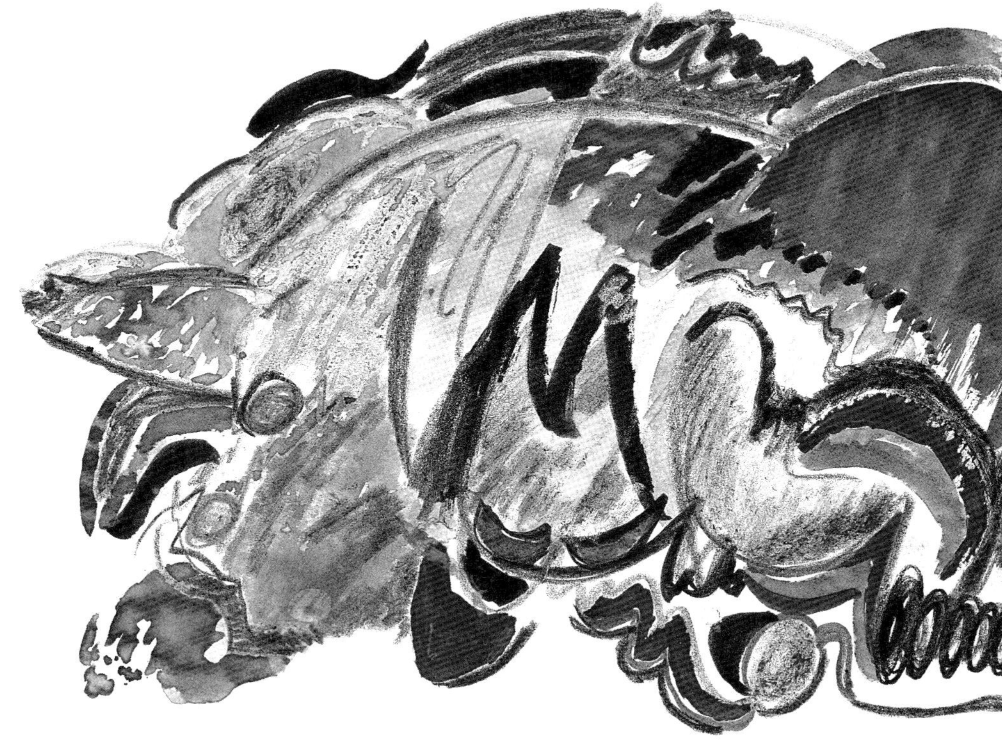

The challenge, therefore, from business to arts education is embodied within the overall challenge to the education system as identified by the secretary of labor's study. It must be determined what changes need be made to teaching methods and curricula in order that the eight foundation and competency skills are achieved for each student. And, although we in business sometimes see ourselves as the primary customers of elementary and secondary education, it is not for business to determine school curriculum content.

Nonetheless, those of us in business believe that education reform should start from, and build on, what people need to know and do in nonschool settings. Schools should not be making distinctions between knowing and doing, or between what we think with our heads and what we make with our hands, or between abstract and applied learning. And herein lies the most powerful argument for the role of the arts in the reform of education. The study of the arts provides an opportunity to learn how to work with ideas, with knowledge, and with information. This has a useful application throughout a lifetime.

Recent studies indicate that most students flourish when knowledge is conveyed in an applied rather than a theoretical setting. Through art, children learn to learn. Because art is, by and large, a hands-on activity, it holds the promise of increasing the learning ability of our future work force.

In his autobiography, Walter Chrysler, automobile company founder, wrote of his apprenticeship, "My fingers were an intake valve through which my mental reservoir was being filled. Of course, my eyes and ears were helping in the process, but what I learned with my fingers and my eyes together I seemed never to forget." What is arts education if not what you learn with your fingers and your eyes together? And how could anyone, especially a businessperson today, miss the connection between arts education and the modern world of work?

There are engineers who say that invention, the conversion of an idea to an artifact, is more the product of art than of science. To design is to invent. The creative genius of America is the result of our investment in our creativity. Our large businesses depend upon it, and our small businesses will surely close their doors if they can't compete through innovation.

Yet, despite all of this evidence, few business leaders put a high priority on arts education as a key element of education reform. This is because, historically, too much of arts education has been separate and focused on training tomorrow's artists and arts teachers. For today's front-line worker, this emphasis is elitist or, at best, extraneous. The business challenge to arts educators is to find creative ways of focusing the arts curriculum on *all* students in the new world of a reformed twenty-first century educational system. The bywords of arts educators should be *relevance* and *interdisciplinary participation*, and the essential tools should be teamwork, enthusiasm, and egalitarianism.

The radical reformation of public education has only just begun. We have only begun to set national standards in core academic subjects as well as in the arts. We have yet to begin the difficult process of driving those standards into all 83,000 of our public schools.

But, if there were ever a community perfectly equipped to meet our educational challenge, it is that of the creative arts. The arts break new ground every day and imagine and produce the unimaginable. If arts educators were to add the integration of the arts into public education reform, then education, business, and political leaders doubtlessly would respond. The time to make it so is now.

And herein lies the most powerful argument for the role of the arts in the reform of education. The study of the arts provides an opportunity to learn how to work with ideas, with knowledge, and with information. This has a useful application throughout a lifetime.

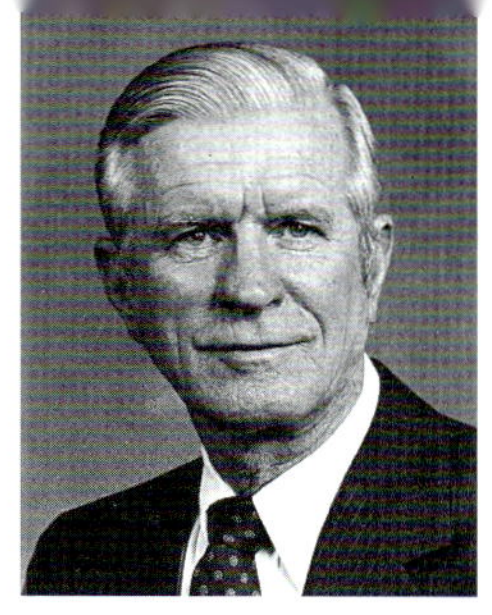

The Challenge of Political Priorities to Arts Education

WILLIAM W. STATON, *Member, North Carolina State Senate*

A few years ago, a legislative study committee of the North Carolina General Assembly was charged with assessing the effect of tourism, historic preservation, and the arts on the state's economy. Public hearings were held throughout the state, and the resulting report concluded that these three activities *were* important to the economic health of North Carolina. After the report was filed, it was declared by legislative enactment that the state of North Carolina would seek to improve the quality of life for its citizens through the arts. This principle has become one of the basic elements of North Carolina's economic development policy.

In recognizing the arts as a means to improve the quality of life, one can quite naturally turn to the issue of arts education as a catalyst for national education reform. In North Carolina, increased media coverage comparing the achievement level of its students with that of students in other states and other countries caused the general population to authorize the state to do whatever is required to improve

performance and to do it as quickly and economically as possible. While there is disagreement within the state as to how this goal can best be met, there is consensus about the degree of reform being sought. "Kicking around the edges" will not result in the level of improvement that North Carolinians are demanding.

There are two ways in which to look at reform as it affects education. The dictionary gives the first definition of reform as "to improve by alteration, correction of error, or removal of defect," which would imply making changes in an education system that already exists. This is the view behind what appears to be the conventional education-reform wisdom. But the second definition given is "to be formed again." This would imply conceiving of an entirely different system of education.

Education reform in the state of North Carolina provides some interesting lessons for those who would attempt to conceive of a new way of viewing educational systems. In North Carolina, as a result of the Elementary and Secondary School Reform Act of 1984, the state's Department of Public Instruction engaged in an extensive audit and revision of the curriculum throughout the summer and fall of that same year. The resulting North Carolina Standard Course of Study

and the North Carolina Competency-Based Curriculum created a detailed and integrated basic course of study for all subjects at all grade levels. In response to constituent demands, the general assembly fully financed the program.

At the very heart of the legislation was the desire to equalize educational opportunities for all North Carolina students, regardless of where in the state they resided. The state confronted the fact that, within the educational system, some of the major differences between the "haves" and "have nots" were in the instructional programs such as second languages and arts education. The Standard Course of Study has made a difference in North Carolina by equalizing access to such programs. In this instance, North Carolina dealt with education reform in the traditional manner of improvement "by alteration, correction of error, and removal of defect."

But, despite the importance of additions to the curriculum, increased numbers of teachers, and more money for educational supplies and materials, these improvements alone are insufficient to achieve the level of improvement deemed necessary for North Carolina students to compete in the world's marketplace. Educators and politicians must be prepared to make the hard decisions about the way we use our resources. It is around these issues that we must do our most creative and innovative thinking if we are to get the job done.

If the debate on education reform continues to focus simply on which subjects of the curriculum are the most important, and how many minutes of the school day must be devoted to each in descending order of importance, we will miss the opportunity for education "to be formed again." The big question is not what we teach, but *how* we teach. And we should care about the kind of people our students will be once they leave the school system. If we can come to some agreement on these questions, we can then look at curriculum as a way to achieve those goals.

In North Carolina, after passage of the basic education program, the state legislature began hearing complaints about the curriculum being too full to work into the school day. So, within the state, we again had the great curriculum debate. And this is where we are today. This is what happens when people cannot conceive of doing things differently. Too many educators are reluctant to make changes in their methods. If integrated teaching is to work, then educators must let go of their sacred schedules in which x number of minutes is devoted to a single subject in isolation from other subjects. We must be innovative, and we must be flexible.

The North Carolina legislature has declared that it believes all children can learn. If we are to teach all children, then we must accept the fact that not all children learn in the same way or at the same rate. Schools must change to accommodate differences among our students. The arts provide models for this kind of education, but their effectiveness has not been well articulated. It must be demonstrated that arts education is flexible enough to fit into the many different patterns that educators may use as their primary methods of instructional delivery. For example, if a school administration decides to teach based on thematic units, then it should build arts education into those themes. If a school decides to follow an outcome-based design, then it should clearly demonstrate how the arts can help students reach those outcomes. In the education reform debate, we must focus on how the arts foster learning in all children. To win the political debate, we must not argue for the arts in isolation from other subjects but, rather, argue for the arts in relation to other subjects.

Across the country there is much constituent support for challenging students to a greater degree. There is recognition that schools need to teach creative and critical thinking skills, encourage independent thinking, and foster self-confidence to raise the can-do attitude that has been so essential to the development of our great country. While, of course, business and industry are seeking employees who can read and write, they also seek people who are creative, innovative, flexible, and able to envision alternative solutions to problems.

Second only to the question of the economy, the issue of education reform is the most important issue of our time. It is constituent-driven at the local, state, and national levels. If arts educators fail to recognize this, then the push to reform education will fail.

Conference
Summaries

Achieving National Education Reform:
Arts Education as Catalyst

San Francisco, California
February 4–6, 1993

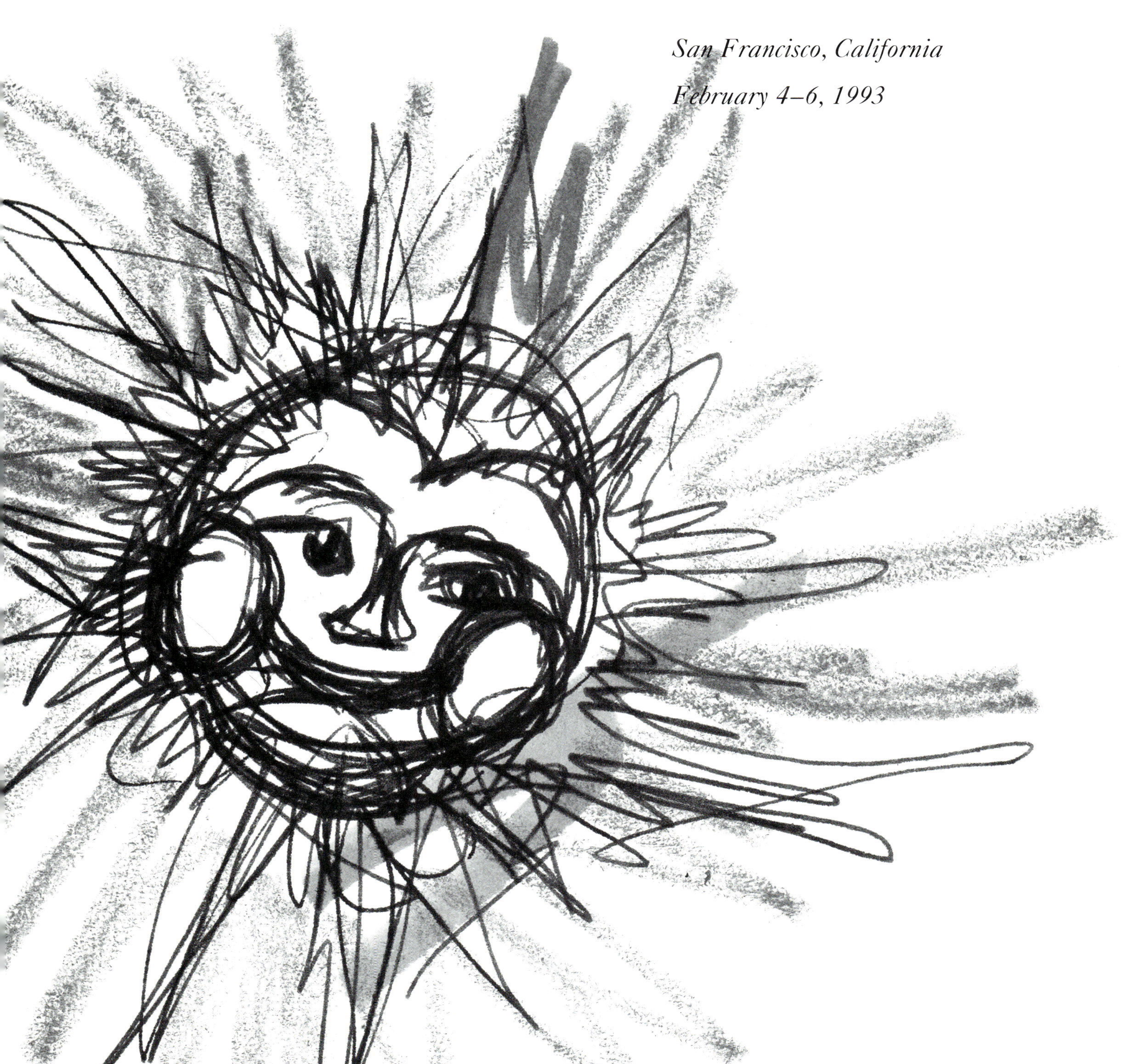

Speaker:

LEILANI LATTIN DUKE, *Director, Getty Center for Education in the Arts*

The arts play a critical and indispensable role in both education and education reform. To illustrate this too-frequently neglected point, LEILANI LATTIN DUKE presented a segment from "The Art of Learning," a one-hour program from The Learning Channel's Teacher TV series. The program demonstrated how arts education is vital to the learning process: facility in the arts enables students to solve problems, take appropriate risks, think creatively, and reason critically. These are among the skills children must have if they are to grow up to be successful adults.

Furthermore, "the arts are not only basic to learning, they are basic learning," said Duke. At the Getty's first national education conference in 1987, concerns were voiced that a holistic curriculum would produce a "Betty Crocker recipe" for arts education, in which other subjects overshadowed the arts. Instead, many remarkable arts education programs have emerged to function as "guiding lights" for other subjects.

Formidable challenges face our education system as the twenty-first century approaches. They grow out of an increasingly multi-cultural society in which emerging technologies constantly change the ways we communicate. New modes of communication alter both the workplace and citizens' interactions with government and society. On-line database systems and CD-ROM technology have the potential to reshape the very nature of the classroom and the ways children learn. Arts educators must keep this in mind while pursuing their education reform goals.

Duke summed up her remarks by stating that the arts can be a powerful catalyst to education reform if they promote the achievement of five key goals: interdisciplinary learning, multicultural understanding, enhanced teaching through the use of new technologies, access and equity in learning, and the development of more revealing assessment techniques. Noting that, with more than 1,500 registrants, this fourth Getty Center for Education in the Arts national conference was the largest yet, Duke maintained that the participation of such a broad and influential array of education professionals indicated that "the time is right for change": The arts must be recognized as a full partner in America's education system.

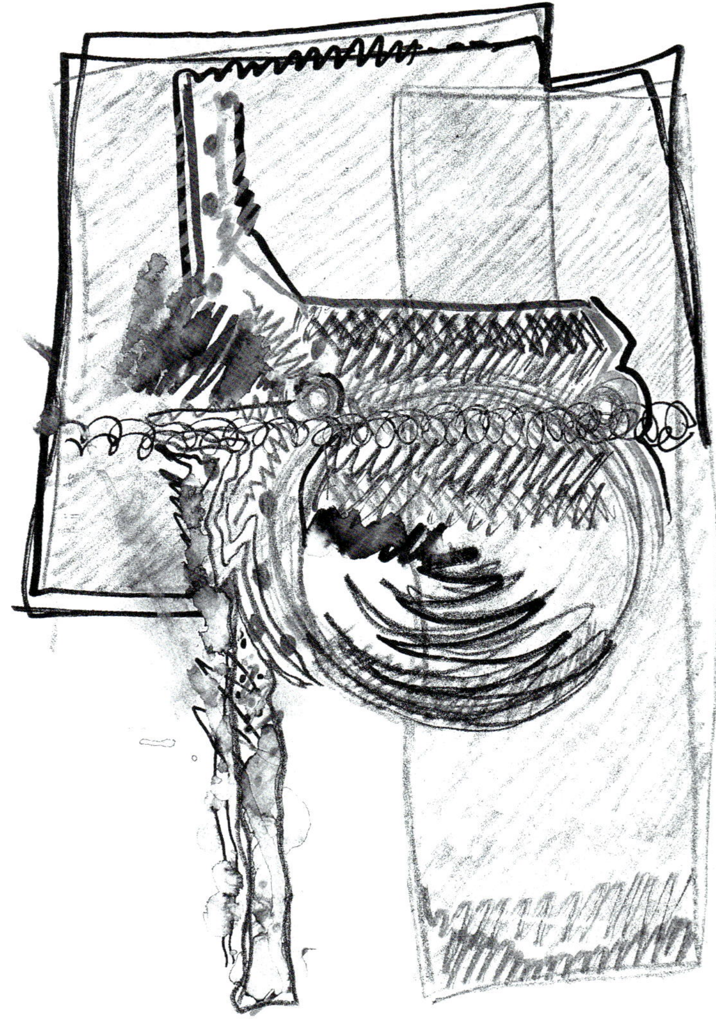

Keynote Address: Education Reform in and through the Arts

Speaker:

GORDON M. AMBACH, *Executive Director, Council of Chief State School Officers*

Introducer:

VALSIN A. MARMILLION, *President, Pacific Visions Communications, Inc.*

"Why is there such a loud cry for education reform?" asked VALSIN MARMILLION in the video "*Why Are the Arts Essential to Education Reform?*" This video, shown before Gordon Ambach's keynote address and introduced by Marmillion, documents an unrehearsed focus-group conversation among parents and teachers as well as government, business, and industry leaders. Discussants agreed that, to be prepared for the twenty-first century, students must have the critical-thinking skills that education in the arts develops and that the arts must be incorporated into an integrated curriculum. Despite their significance for creative thinking and problem solving in the information age, however, the arts are currently marginalized. Arts organizations will thus have to aggressively communicate the tangible benefits of the arts if they are to gain a substantial place in the curriculum. The arts community must take a strong position in the education reform debate and on the difficult issues surrounding changing cultural values.

In his keynote address, GORDON AMBACH recalled the sign over the desk of Clinton campaign manager James Carville that read, "The economy, stupid." It served as a reminder of the campaign's central message, and Ambach proposed that the arts community use a similar motto to reinforce its message to the public: "The arts, stupid."

"Learning in the arts is central to the education of every student in America," Ambach declared. Such learning can play a critical role in five overall education-reform strategies:

1. establishing new standards and goals for learning;
2. developing new performance assessments for measuring progress toward those standards;
3. achieving higher-order thinking skills, which are interdisciplinary and require self-discipline;
4. capturing the wizardry of technology for teaching and learning; and
5. celebrating both the diversity and the unity of American culture.

Struggling to agree on standards and goals is a positive activity that stimulates renewal in the arts community and keeps the arts on the public agenda. Standards should denote the "best practice," as they do in the business world, rather than merely establish minimums. And they should be framed in an international context. As America's long-held preference for standardized tests wanes, interest is increasing in "real demonstrations of what students are learning." The arts, with their portfolio, audition, and performance-assessment models, can play a leadership role in reshaping testing in other subjects.

Learning in and through the arts is an essential vehicle for developing higher-order thinking skills and students' capacities to understand and use technologies that rely on image, sound, and data to communicate. The arts display what is common to all American cultures and enable us to explore and perpetuate the diversity of America's cultural roots. Ambach concluded by quoting Maxine Greene: "Engagement through the arts provides the key to the door of the imaginative life and that means the key to untapped possibility, to a sense of what is not yet."

Strong Arts, Strong Schools

Speaker:

CHARLES FOWLER, *Director,*
National Cultural Resources, Inc.

The arts function as a transforming agent in public schooling. In forty years of observing the American school system, CHARLES FOWLER has found that the best schools are those with the best arts programs: "Excellence in education and excellence in the arts seem to go hand in hand." Arts education instills divergent rather than convergent modes of thinking, allowing students to "create their own world rather than replicate someone else's." Study of the arts develops the craftsmanship and aesthetic judgment that are essential for a competent work force. "The arts require students to apply standards to their own work, to be self-critical, and to be able to self-correct." And they introduce us to ideas and perceptions that would otherwise be inaccessible.

Through their capacity to provide insight and wisdom, "the arts add significantly to the dimensions of general education." The arts are inherently enlightening, without overloading us with information—which is not the same as meaning. "The arts give us wisdom, not data," Fowler stressed. Humans must develop every possible method of responding to and investigating our world, for science, mathematics, and history convey only part of the reality of our universe. The arts "enlighten our understanding, making it deeper and more comprehensive."

By facilitating human communication within and across cultures, the arts "articulate our own very special sense of being." Fowler believes "this is a near miracle, because as soon as we have a glimpse of other people's humanity, we have crossed the cultural chasm that separates us." We should thus value the arts for their relationship to what is most precious to us: our emotional and spiritual well-being. "The human spirit, in all of its manifestations, is central to the arts."

Fowler argued that "the arts *are* general education, and they should be taught *as* general education." In the best schools, they are incorporated as valued components of learning. Schools that ignore the arts are cold and desolate places, creating a generation less civilized than it should be. "The arts must be part of a basic education," Fowler insisted, "not for art's sake, but for humanity's sake."

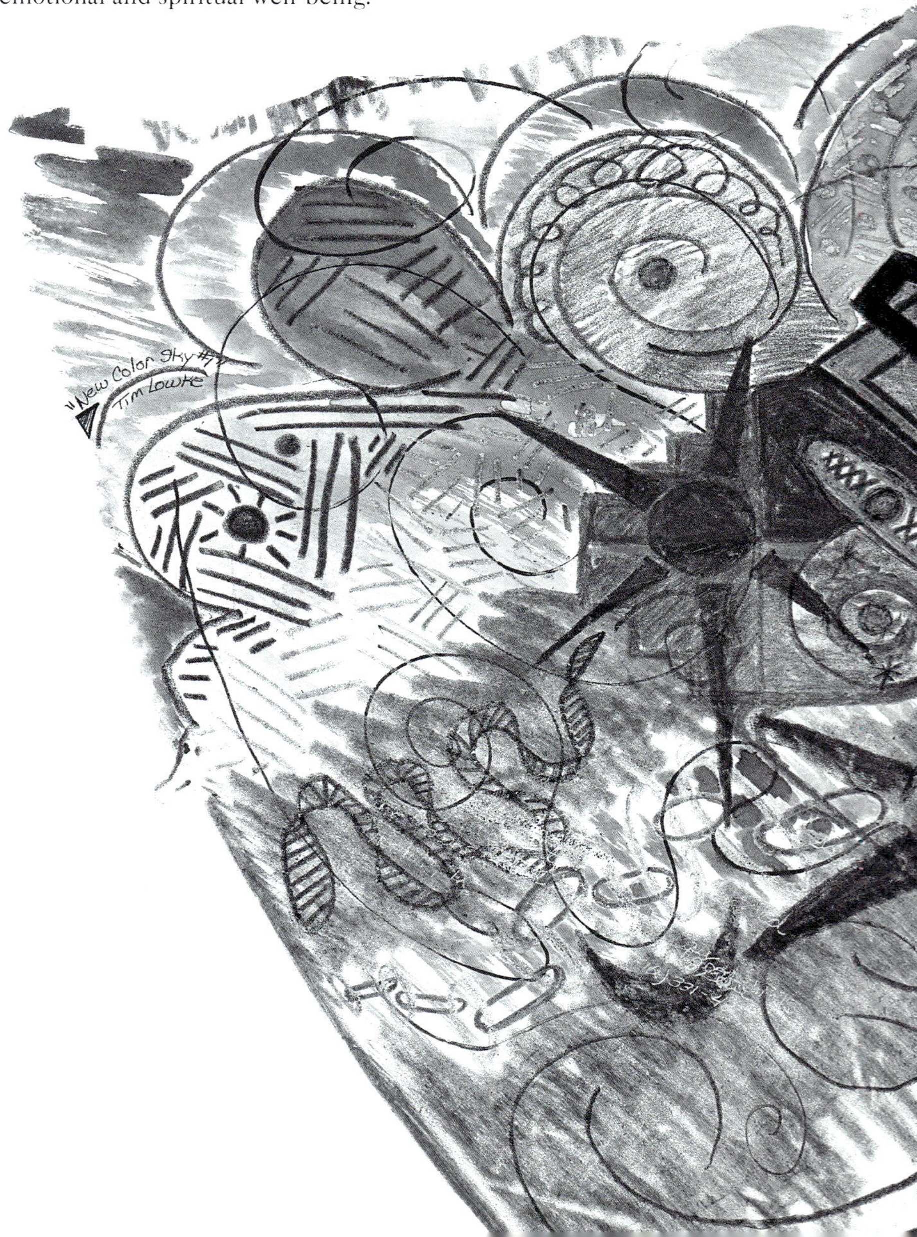

Challenges Facing Arts Education:

The Challenge from Business to Arts Education

Speakers:

WILLIAM H. KOLBERG, *President, National Alliance of Business*

DENIS P. DOYLE, *Senior Fellow, Hudson Institute*

Moderator:

RICHARD S. GURIN, *President and Chief Executive Officer, Binney & Smith, Inc.*

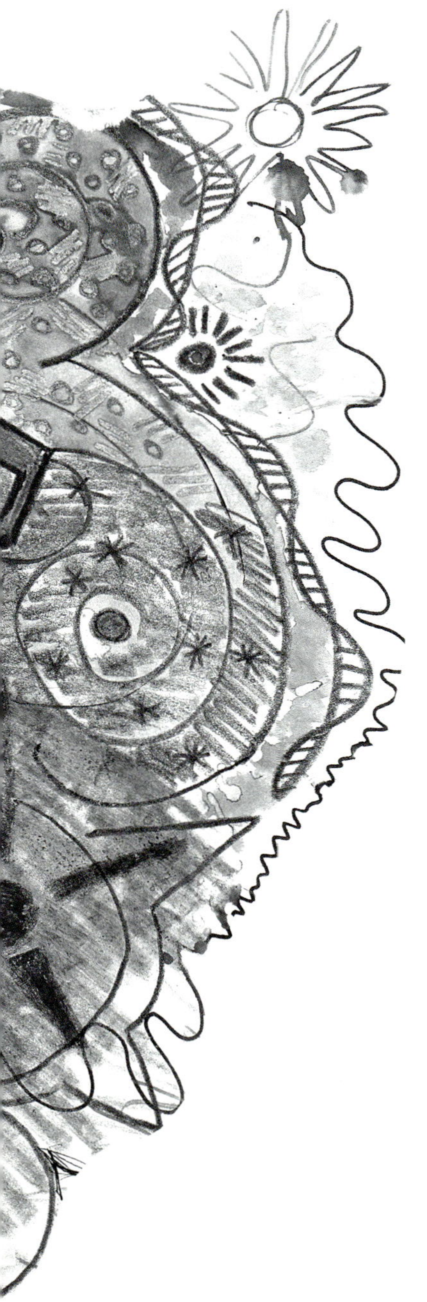

To reach the business community, RICHARD GURIN advised arts educators and artists to demonstrate how the arts enhance business competitiveness. That is, "show business how you can help us. *You* must be the catalyst for change because competitiveness is the only thing that turns the business community on." He acknowledged that, to survive in the current rapidly changing economic climate, "businesses need creative vision and strong leadership at a world-class level," both of which can be enhanced with study in the arts.

WILLIAM KOLBERG informed conference participants that the National Alliance of Business passionately believes that public education must undergo a radical reformation if it is to keep pace with the rapid changes in today's technology and the modern workplace. To prepare our children to thrive in a world of dramatic change, we must use "equally revolutionary" methods.

American business can no longer rely on mass production or afford to be satisfied with "front-line" workers who may be functionally illiterate. Every worker must be a creative problem solver. Unfortunately, American students consistently rank last or near last in international math, science, and biology competitions, and our high school dropout rate is 25 percent or higher. The United States is the only country in the industrialized world that has not set national education standards.

A two-year study commissioned by the secretary of labor identified three groups of skills business needs from entry-level workers:

1. reading, writing, and math;
2. creative thinking, decision-making, and problem-solving abilities, including knowing how to learn; and
3. personal qualities such as responsibility, self-esteem, integrity, honesty, and sociability — a far broader range of skills than business professionals had ever before considered.

Moreover, argued Kolberg, education must foster in students the competencies needed by business in resource management; interpersonal interaction, including teamwork and leadership; information acquisition and application;

system maintenance, including the abilities to understand and manage; and technical and application skills. The most powerful argument for including the arts in the campaign for education reform is that they enable students to work with complex ideas and teach children to "learn to learn."

DENIS DOYLE recalled Alfred North Whitehead's definition of art as "in its broadest sense, civilization" and debunked the notion that art is elitist. "It is the least elitist activity in which we engage as a people. Art is accessible to everyone." Further, the arts have fueled many of the current reforms in education, as evidenced by multimedia displays that are "breathtaking in appearance as well as impressive in intellectual depth." By contrast, the slender list of "modern" educational technologies is headed by the lead pencil, the overhead projector, and the public address system. Deeply rooted in the arts, the new educational technology will transcend "the dehumanizing technology" of the machine-scored true/false examination.

The arts annually generate $173 billion in income, or 3.3 percent of our gross national product (GNP), and employment in the arts sector is growing at a rate of 6 percent per year. Arts-oriented sectors of the economy, such as photography, account for 5.8 percent of the GNP, and are growing at an even faster annual rate of 6.7 percent. This figure is roughly equal either to the amount the United States spends on elementary and secondary education or a third of the nation's health care expenditures. These figures, Doyle concluded, prove that "the arts play an extraordinary role in the modern economy."

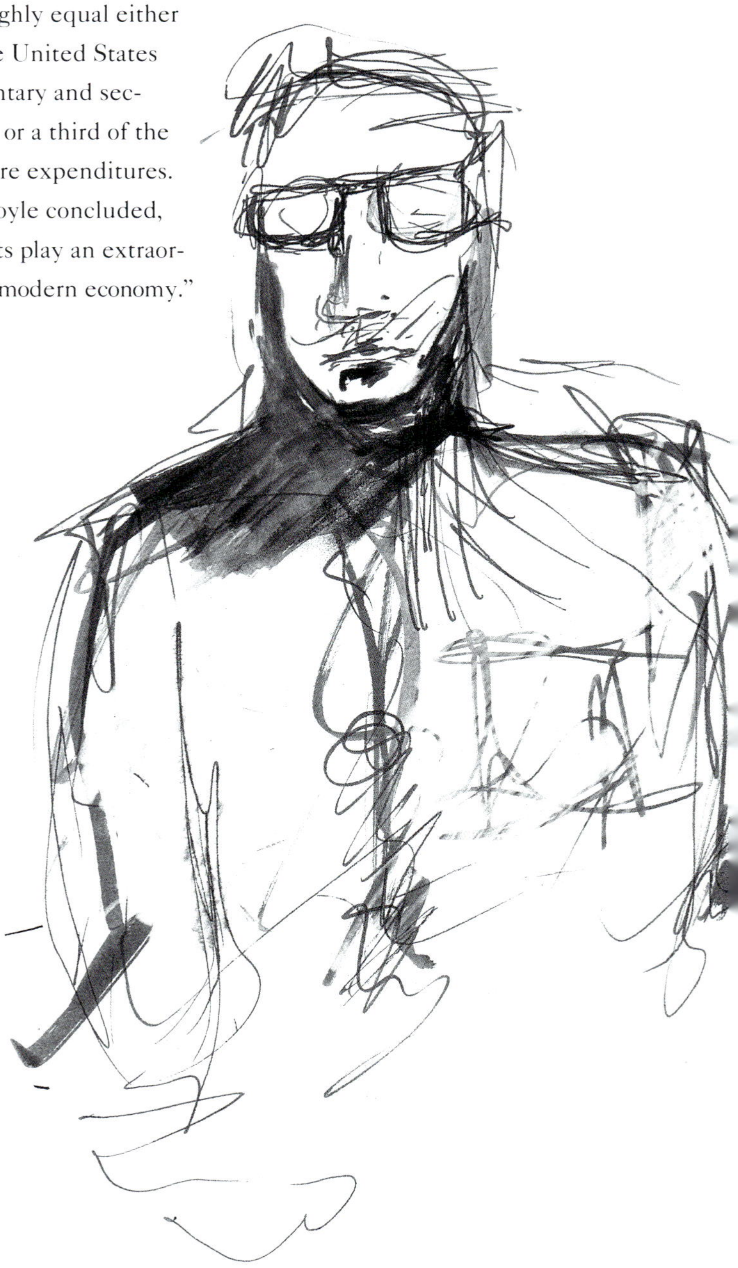

Challenges Facing Arts Education:

The Challenge from Education to Arts Education

Speakers:

RAMON C. CORTINES, *Assistant Secretary Designate for Intergovernmental and Interagency Affairs, and Assistant Secretary Designate for Human Resources and Administration, U.S. Department of Education*
BENJAMIN O. CANADA, *Superintendent, Jackson (Mississippi) Public School District*

Moderator:

A. GRAHAM DOWN, *President, Council for Basic Education*

The "unbridled utilitarianism" that colors public policy in the United States has not been sufficiently addressed, announced GRAHAM DOWN. Despite the opinion of "myopic minimalists" who champion a return to the "basics," the arts are not an expendable frill.

RAMON CORTINES identified eight challenges to the arts community. He suggested that arts administrators and educators must:

1. use the arts to facilitate the transition of young children to the formal education process in Head Start and kindergarten programs — in higher grades, encourage arts partnerships, such as those currently employed by innovative social science and literature teachers, across all disciplines;

2. develop a "tapestry of education" that weaves the threads of culture, history, politics, and economics into a framework students can comprehend through art;

3. create partnerships among schools, foundations, businesses, and cultural institutions to defend against funding cuts to the arts and arts education;

4. understand how children grow and develop;

5. build capacities for learning and develop new ways to teach and learn through the use of new technologies;

6. strive for higher values;

7. encourage respect for and participation in education research to improve teaching techniques; and

8. use their own skills and talents as educators to help children grow and develop through art and, in so doing, become contributing citizens.

BENJAMIN CANADA organized his remarks about the challenges to arts education around three concepts: perception, collaboration, and preparation. To illustrate the power of perception, he offered the example of a trip he took through Mississippi while a student at Southern University in Louisiana. Canada and some companions, all African Americans, were stopped by a White sheriff who, feeling a "lack of respect" from the travelers, harassed them. Years later, upon returning to Mississippi to interview for the position of superintendent of the Jackson Public School District, Canada feigned an automobile breakdown to discover if he would be welcomed as a Black man in the city. Almost immediately, he received an offer of assistance from an elderly White man. Had he not tested his earlier experience, a prior perception of Mississippi, "based on an event that occurred thirty years ago, might have kept me from one of the most rewarding experiences of my life."

Turning to collaboration, Canada recalled threats of funding cuts by the governor to the Jackson school system's "music mentors" program, a partnership with the Mississippi Symphony. Canada met with the governor to emphasize the importance of arts education, and funding for the mentor program was restored. Similar collaborations between educators and decision makers are desperately needed.

Finally, Canada addressed the preparation of arts educators. In an environment in which funders, performers, arts patrons, businesses, and other "outsiders" are making decisions about curricula, arts educators must carefully examine "what needs to be taught and who needs to teach it." Canada argued for alternative certification to allow individuals with outstanding artistic skills but no formal training to teach in a classroom.

Challenges Facing Arts Education:

The Challenge of Political Priorities to Arts Education

Speakers:
WILLIAM W. STATON, *Member, North Carolina State Senate*
WILLIAM F. MARX, *Fiscal Analyst (Education), Ways and Means Committee, Minnesota House of Representatives*
Moderator:
CISCO MCSORLEY, *Member, New Mexico House of Representatives*

Politicians find it difficult to discern their constituents' expectations in regard to arts education, reported CISCO MCSORLEY. In Albuquerque, for instance, many parents are removing their children from public schools and placing them in private schools, which are experiencing double- and even triple-digit growth. The "lack of the arts" in public schools is one of five primary reasons these parents give for their actions. Yet, other parents, apparently influenced by the back-to-basics rhetoric of the 1980s, still insist that the arts are nothing more than educational frills. McSorley called for a renewal, in the political realm, of the emphasis on the arts in public education. "How could Plato have understood his world," he asked, "if he did not understand the arts of his time?" Furthermore, McSorley pointed to the vital interconnections in education among the arts and sciences — something that many of the great figures of history, such as Leonardo da Vinci, have clearly understood.

Several years ago, WILLIAM STATON served as cochairman of a legislative study committee of the North Carolina General Assembly charged with assessing the effect of tourism, historic preservation, and the arts on the state's economy. The committee's final report concluded that all were vital to the state's economic health, and the assembly passed legislation making it a matter of public policy that North Carolina improve the quality of citizens' lives through the arts. That principle has come to be one of the basic elements of the state's economic development policy.

Yet, change in the state's approach to education to reflect that emphasis on the arts has not been quick in coming. Constituents' expectations in regard to education reform seem to be rather simple, according to Staton: "Do whatever is required to ensure improvement and do it as quickly and as economically as possible." There is, however, "a tremendous difference of opinion about how to achieve results." All that is clear at the moment to education reformers in the political process is that "significant and drastic education reforms are necessary if we are to meet the demands of our constituents."

The idea that the arts are "frills" disturbs Staton, especially because a community's well-being and fiscal stability are directly linked to the arts. While there is a place in political debate to address curricular aspects of education reform, overemphasis on this issue

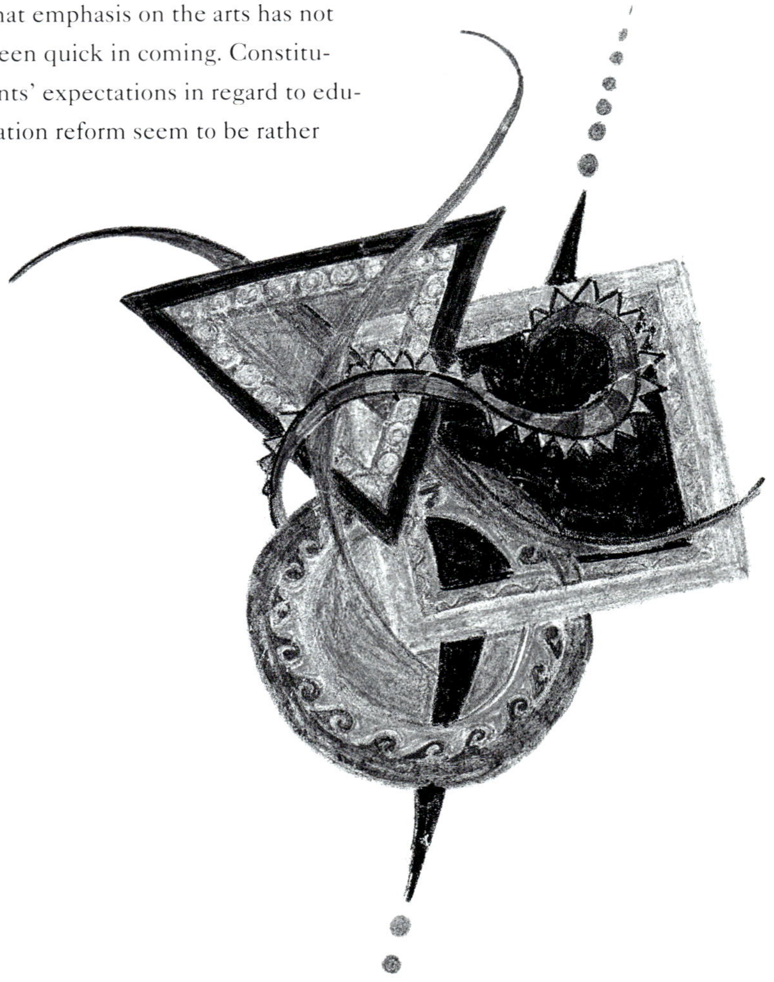

may result in "missing the big question, which is not *what* we teach but *how* we teach." Not only do "the arts help to accomplish so many of the things that we identify with a good education," but an arts education can serve as a model for teaching those children who cannot learn as others do. Staton urged advocates to focus on the ways the arts foster learning in all children and stress the arts' intrinsic connection to other issues. After the economy, education reform is the most important concern of our time. If arts educators fail to recognize this as a burning political issue, "then arts educators will fail in their attempt to achieve education reform."

WILLIAM MARX noted that education is moving from the measurement of "inputs" and hours of instruction toward the measurement of outcomes. Driving this change is the realization among educators that the emphasis in education should be on what students learn and not on how much time they spend on a particular subject, how they are taught, or who teaches them. Educators must move beyond "component parts" to define what students *really* need to learn, and then they must work together to devise plans to achieve their goals.

Marx posed a series of questions that the field will need to address. To what extent can arts education be used to help students meet overall education goals?

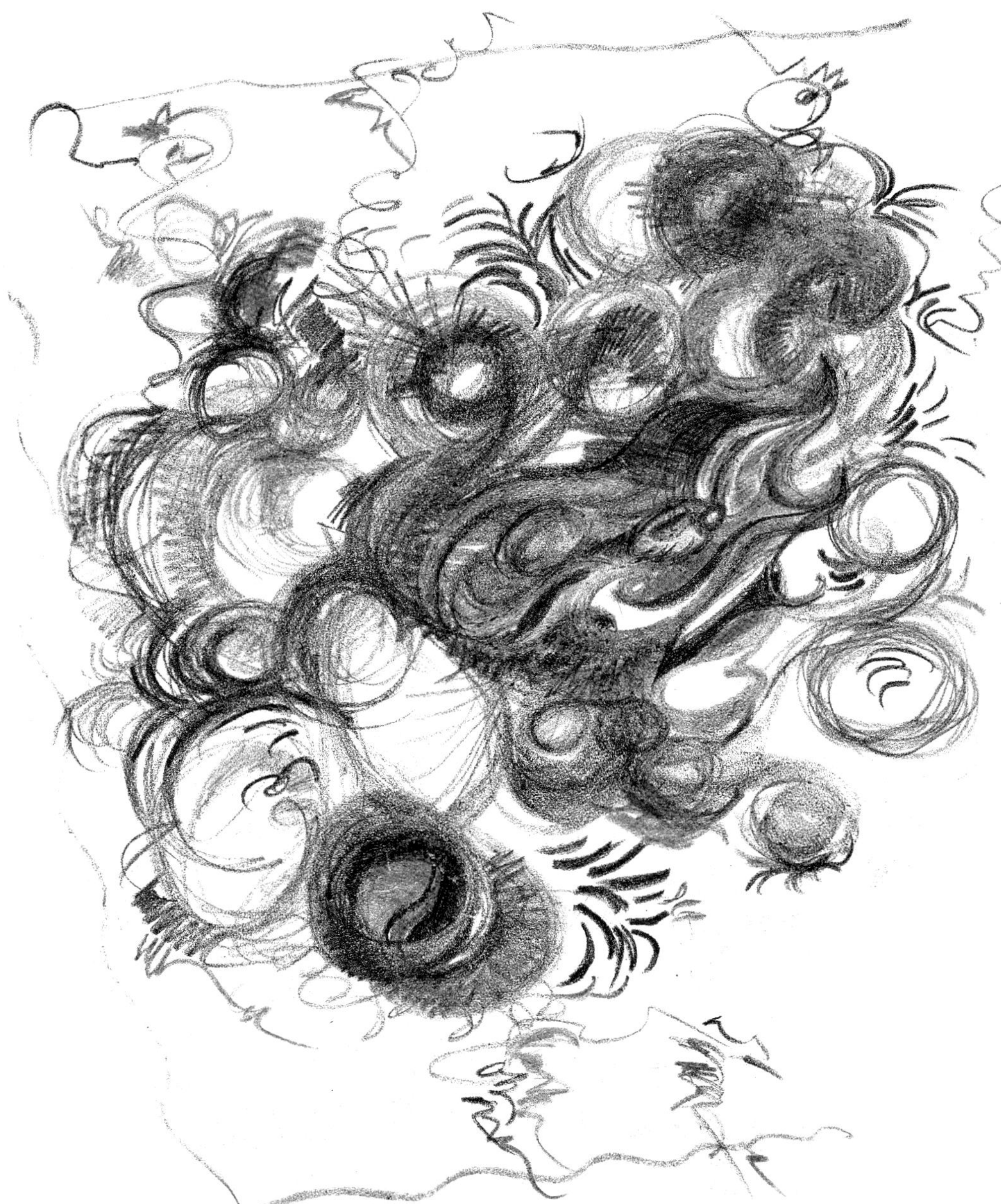

Should the arts be taught as disciplines in their own right? Or, should teachers use the arts as a vehicle for teaching other, higher-order skills? As arts education becomes a vehicle to meet overall goals, might education in the arts per se be sacrificed? It will be clear that the necessary change has occurred, according to Marx, when educators are finally willing to validate learning whenever and wherever it occurs (for example, acknowledge that math concepts can be learned in music class).

"Arts education provides an opportunity for active engagement in education and endless opportunities to promote creativity." Marx concluded: "Arts education must be part of the education mainstream." Therefore, discussions on graduation requirements must include arts educators. The knowledge and insight of arts educators, he continued, will benefit the entire educational process.

Speakers:

JAMES A. MECKLENBURGER, *President, The Mecklenburger Group*

NANCY HECHINGER, *Founding Partner, The Edison Project*

BERNARD J. LUSKIN, *President, Philips Interactive Media of America*

Moderator:

STEPHEN M. DOBBS, *President and Chief Executive Officer, Marin Community Foundation*

Few things in our modern world change so quickly as technology, communications technology in particular. The arts are vital, asserted STEPHEN DOBBS, in providing the "grammar and syntax" that we need to understand and fully appreciate the languages of our new electronic technologies. The interaction between the arts and communications technology points to the importance of the arts in education in general: The arts provide students in all disciplines with a "sense of experience, of intuition, of immediacy, and of awe and wonder."

American education is at a crossroads: Shall we continue to employ educational technology designed in and for the nineteenth century or move into the twenty-first with the myriad new technologies that may entirely alter education as we know it? "Two centuries ago," commented JAMES MECKLENBURGER, "this nation committed itself to an incredible dream — universal education." By the close of the nineteenth-century, educators' attempts to fulfill that dream had become an unprecedented technological adventure. The technology that produced the textbook was revolutionary in its time as was the willpower evident in building a schoolhouse in every community. Providing a course of study with textbooks and teachers to match was a civic movement of grand scale with few historical precedents.

But the spirit of technological adventure that launched the system has not been sustained. That once-adventurous, and now outmoded, nineteenth-century system has persisted into the late twentieth century. Modern educators, lamented Mecklenburger, have neglected to use new information technology to transform the education process. Decades after their invention, even the usually ubiquitous television, telephone, and VCR — much less the computer — are rarities in most classrooms.

To rekindle the spirit of technological adventure in our time, educators must "consider the educational innovations and benefits of putting telephones and modems in classrooms. Imagine the research students could do. Give students audiocassette recorders and video cameras. Imagine the projects students could undertake." Furthermore, educators should recognize a parallel system of education that has developed, one that brings talk show hosts such as Phil Donahue and Larry King and the issues, personalities, values, and information of the day into our living rooms. Or consider today's most famous physical education teachers, such as Jane Fonda and Arnold Schwarzenegger. They use videocassettes, the educational technology of *our* times to deliver instruction. And nationwide TV channels — Cable News Network (CNN) and The Discovery Channel, for example — deliver their lessons anywhere.

Mecklenburger chided educators for not fully realizing the educational possibilities of Channel One, a nationwide educational TV channel that is made possible through advertising. Channel One delivers its lessons to any location with a TV — "not just to a place called 'school.'" Such developments point to how far we can go, said Mecklenburger, "if we choose to get out of the box called the 'classroom' and take advantage of the technologies of the twentieth century." And these technologies are growing at wondrous rates. In the near future, cable hook-ups will handle 500 channels instead of the current 50. That advance is dwarfed by Time-Warner's recent announcement of a forthcoming full-service cable network that will handle nearly all electronic communications functions, including telephone service.

Mecklenburger acknowledged that technology is not an education panacea. However, he argued that a "fundamental opportunity is at hand for educators if we understand that education does not stop at the school walls or even require those walls. The new technology is ours for the taking, and I wish us Godspeed."

The Edison Project, reported NANCY HECHINGER, is designing and building a national system of private schools that will deliver quality education for the same price as the public system. The Project, which will encompass kindergarten through the second year of college, plans to open its first group of schools by 1996, with as many as one thousand in operation by 2010.

The Project's seven-member core team has visited schools across the country, analyzing them with an eye toward creating a wholly new approach to education. The team questions everything, from the need for classrooms to spelling bees. The Catch-22 of current public education, it seems, is that the rules prevent innovation. Edison schools will operate instead on a "Catch-23" premise, focusing on "what you could do if you could do what you wanted," and Hechinger challenged the audience to do the same.

Citing positive correlations between high SAT scores and instruction in music and art, Hechinger explained that every child in an Edison school will learn to play a musical instrument, and the school will sing together as a community. Students will study the visual arts and music as often as they study math. Edison schools, however, will not treat the arts as isolated subjects. Valued for their ability to inspire and "provide a fertile ground for kids to explore," the arts will be woven through the curriculum.

Hechinger reminded the audience that much of the world's great art began as instruction. She cited Bach's *Well-Tempered Clavier*, written for his six-year-old son to break up the tedium of playing scales. The Edison Project intends to do the same with math, science, and history, inventing "a well-tempered curriculum." Hechinger hoped that the Project's teachers would think of themselves not only as coaches and guides, as many conventional educators do now, but also as maestros and mentors.

While the Edison Project will bring electronic technology into every aspect of school activity, Hechinger voiced her skepticism of the "multimedia disease" that is spreading throughout the education community. It is not dazzling technology that makes a great school, she asserted, but rather the students, teachers, curriculum, and the "energy of the culture."

Technology is an effective education tool only insofar as it is "as transparent and easy to use as possible." BERNARD LUSKIN, characterizing himself as a populist in regard to education and technology, proclaimed his particular concern about the many students for whom the television set could function as a teacher's assistant and teaching aid.

Luskin demonstrated three compact disc interactive (CD-I) programs produced by his company that run on a self-contained unit that hooks up with a standard television and stereo. "Treasures of the Smithsonian," a program containing 150 artworks that can be individually accessed, allows a user to retrieve the image of a Brancusi sculpture, for example. The user can then zoom in on it to reveal crucial details or rotate it 360 degrees in order to view it from all angles. "Art of the Czars" profiles the vast collections of Russia's rulers, including the ill-fated Nicholas II. Lastly, Luskin presented a CD-I, employing a cutting-edge interface, that holds a twenty-six volume encyclopedia.

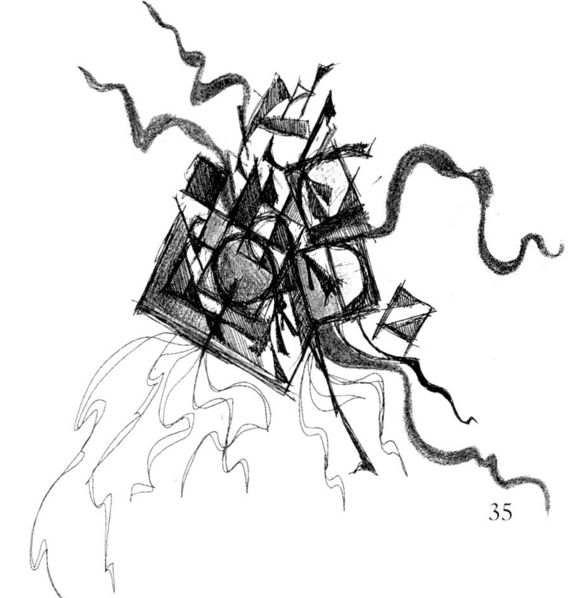

Arts Education as a Catalyst to Reform: Interdisciplinary Learning

Speakers:

DAVID L. BACH, *Executive Director, Minnesota Alliance for Arts in Education*

CATHERINE LEFFLER, *Instructor, Encino Elementary School, Los Angeles Unified School District*

The burgeoning interest in interdisciplinary learning offers a crucial opportunity for positioning the arts at the center of education reform. However, "teachers and administrators," lamented DAVID BACH, "still have both feet in the past." Yet, reported Bach, innovation is on the rise. The movement toward interdisciplinary learning in Minnesota, a state with a strong commitment to arts education, has been accompanied by a shift to the new system of outcome-based education. Such a system is oriented toward five exit outcomes that are not discipline specific. Rather, the system focuses on generic skills and abilities that transcend discipline content.

Although Minnesota does not mandate interdisciplinary learning, the state is making efforts to incorporate it into the schools through various pilot programs. For instance, the state-funded Minnesota Center for Arts Education includes a state arts high school for 270 eleventh- and twelfth-grade residential students and a statewide resource program providing services for teachers and students. In its first year, the high school program set up ten interdisciplinary learning goals. Topics used to address these goals included the study of communication elements and structural principles common to the arts and general studies, as well as a comparative study of "ways of knowing." By its second year, the program offered eight distinct programs addressing such topics as cultural transformations, the science of chaos, and "herstory" (as opposed to "history"). The Minnesota Center discovered that the success of interdisciplinary programs depends on several factors, among them the flexibility of teachers, number of students, amount of planning time for teachers, quality of preservice and inservice education, use of participatory teaching and learning strategies, creation of adequate assessment procedures, and the willingness of teachers to relinquish some control of instruction to students. The Minnesota Center for Arts Education has also conducted teacher workshops on interdisciplinary learning and sponsored a statewide focus group of teachers and students.

Among other teacher-training programs in the state is a joint program of the Walker Art Center and the Minneapolis Institute of Arts that began in 1986. Originally called Art Link, this intensive three-week program connects pairs of teachers with museum resources and helps them develop interdisciplinary curricula for their schools. Approximately twenty teachers from all disciplines have participated in the program, now called Muse Arts. SAIL (Strengthening Arts in Learning), a joint venture of the Cook County schools and the Arts Colony in Grand Marais, Minnesota, convenes local artists, community members, teachers, and students to work on specific interdisciplinary themes.

CATHERINE LEFFLER recently attended the first national conference on integrated curriculum, where she encountered a network of teachers involved with an integrated thematic approach to teaching. Leffler cited Howard Gardner's definition of intellgence, which provides a theoretical framework for the development of such a curriculum. She believes Gardner's open definition of intelligence "gives us all a place in the world" because it affirms the potential value of all forms of learning and knowledge, not simply the verbal, mathematical, and logical forms emphasized in traditional education. Music, form, space, movement, emotions, behavior, and relationships are among the many "intelligences" a person employs throughout a lifetime. Significantly, all are called into play in the practice and study of the arts.

Researchers concerned with the nature of intelligence once held that it is the product of a sequential, logic-oriented process. Now, however, many of these researchers have discovered that intelligence is a function of experience and that the mind operates as a pattern-seeking device. That is, nothing is learned in isolation, nor do certain ideas always "naturally" follow from others. Intelligence results from the active networking and grouping of ideas through long-term learning.

The integrated curriculum approach seeks to take advantage of these discoveries. While traditional education training instructs teachers to use a single-subject format, such as history, the integrated approach addresses a number of subjects through a common theme.

Leffler provided an example of an integrated thematic unit, whose theme was the relationship of the late nineteenth-century American artist Frederic Remington and Kicking Bear, a Lakota Indian leader, both of whom painted versions of the Battle of Little Big Horn. The theme was broad enough to encompass a wide range of disciplines, issues, and materials, including American cultural, political, and social history; art history and aesthetics; nineteenth-century technology; Indian culture; the boundary between fine and popular art; and other art of the period, such as Walt Whitman's poetry and the paintings of Winslow Homer and Albert Bierstadt.

Thematic teaching integrates and relates activities and ideas and emphasizes the process of constructing meaning, solving problems, and discovering relationships. Both students and teachers take charge of instruction, and classroom time is allotted in a fluid as opposed to a preset way. Intellectual processes such as interpretation, brainstorming, observing, and synthesizing are stressed.

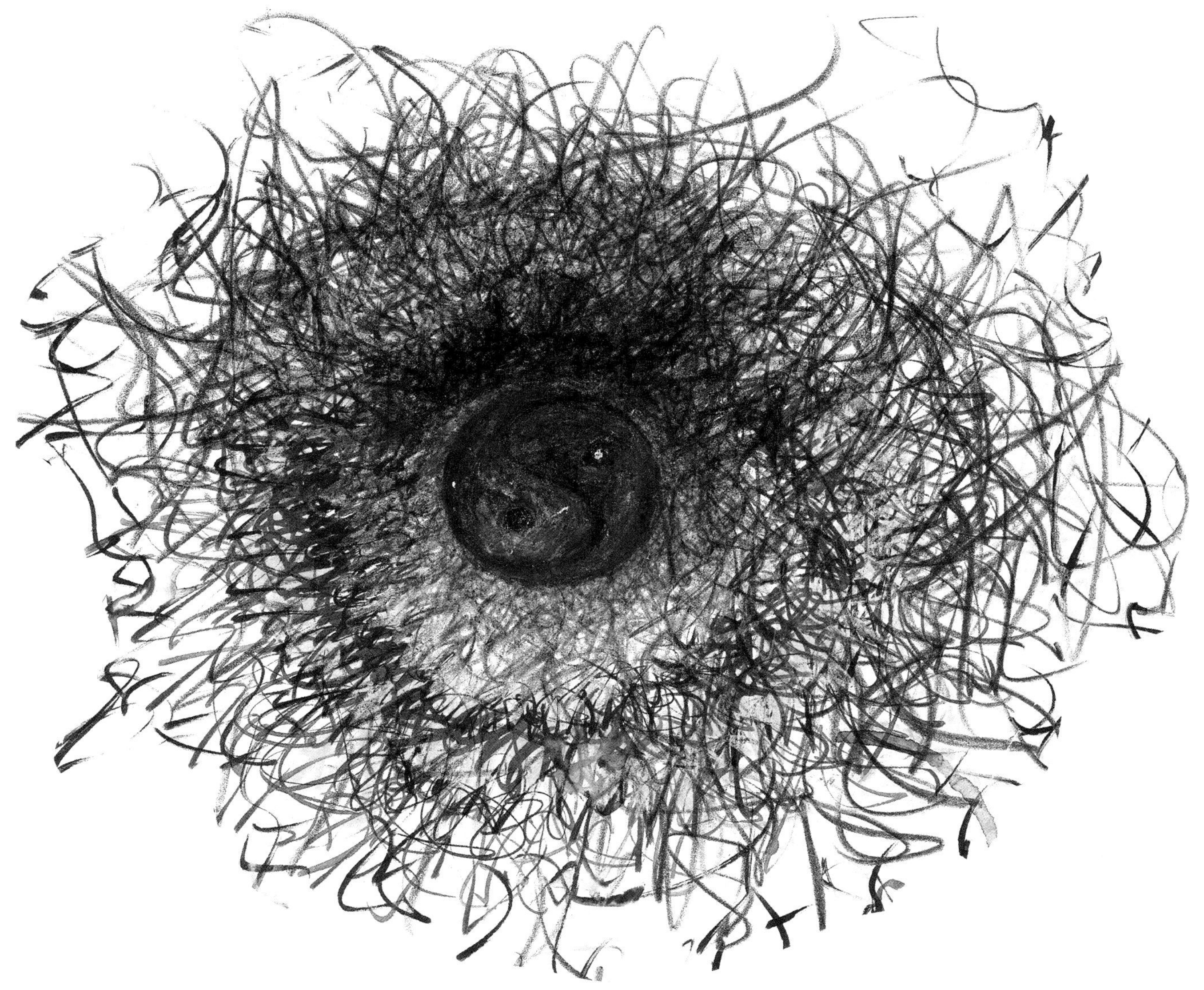

Arts Education as a Catalyst to Reform:
Assessment

Speaker:

RAMSAY W. SELDEN, *Director, State Education Assessment Center, Council of Chief State School Officers*

Standards and assessments are evolving into a fundamentally new concept of schooling. One of the major efforts of the Council of Chief State School Officers has been helping to guide the rethinking of current approaches to assessment in schools, explained RAMSAY SELDEN. Rather than academically evaluating students along a "normal" curve, the new models are based on the belief that all students can rise to high levels of achievement. Instead of ranking students in relation to one another as below or above average, schools are now interested in measuring them against an absolute standard. Furthermore, educators are becoming increasingly committed to formulating specific, systemwide education goals and standards. Finally, a general understanding now exists that schools and teachers, far from being passive factors, have a major impact on student achievement.

The education system has yet to realize the magnitude of these changes. The New Standards Project, being conducted by the University of Pittsburgh and the National Center for Education and the Economy, advocates assessment programs geared to the highest national standards and is committed to the belief that the vast majority of America's students can achieve them. The inauguration of this project marks the beginning of a fundamentally new view of educational psychology and development.

The National Education Goals Panel and the National Council on Educational Standards and Testing (NCEST) have recommended that voluntary standards be developed by the professional community rather than by any federal agency. This reflects the desire for a nationally focused effort as well as sensitivity to decentralization and diversity. The third of the six National Educational Goals, proposed at the 1990 joint education summit of the nation's governors and President Bush, calls for the mastery of high levels of academic subject matter and the development of the minds of U.S. citizens in productive ways. In addition, it confirms the need to develop standards for defining mastery and to establish measures of how school systems are moving toward the goal. NCEST was established to study whether standards are appropriate for American schools; if it is politically, financially, and logistically feasible to have national standards; and if so, what might be the best ways to implement them.

NCEST, formed to address these issues, recommended three types of voluntary standards:

1. content standards defining types of knowledge students should learn in various subjects;

2. performance standards declaring how much of that knowledge is desired; and

3. delivery standards identifying the resources, processes, and facilities that would make it possible for students to reach these standards.

Several national-level assessments have already emerged. These include the New Standards Project, affecting approximately half the students in the country, and the States' Collaborative on Assessment and Standards for Students. The Collaborative consists of approximately twenty-five states assembled by the Council of Chief State School Officers. Their goal is to pool their resources to develop and share new assessment programs designed to meet high standards.

While the arts have thus far been leapfrogged in this issue, the development of arts assessments will contribute to and guide the development of arts education. Selden called for assessments that are supportive of instruction and do not replicate the pressures for high test scores imposed by old-style achievement tests. It is essential to engage the arts education community in the standard-setting process in order to send a compelling message to the public about the importance of arts education as well as to guarantee high-quality assessment programs.

Arts Education as a Catalyst to Reform: Equity and Access

Speakers:

NANCY ROUCHER, *Codirector, Florida Institute for Art Education*
BARBARA GUTHEIL, *Classroom Instructor, Frances K. Sweet Elementary School, St. Lucie County (Florida) School District*

The arts are more than a grade-school discipline for middle-class children. NANCY ROUCHER contended, an arts-based education offers "content, a series of strategies, a new way to teach and learn, and a way of speaking to the human spirit." As such, the arts must be a part of the education of all children, not just those of the middle classes.

Furthermore, arts-based education can benefit those beyond grade-school walls. Roucher described a class of teenage mothers whose teacher, following attendance at a discipline-based arts education institute, had the teenagers make a series of conceptual, symbolic images of their families. These images enabled the students to examine how they saw themselves and others.

Roucher introduced BARBARA GUTHEIL as a teacher of four-year-old at-risk students, many of whom are children of color and of migrant farm workers. Her experience demonstrates how arts-based education can benefit all students, bringing the arts — and exciting learning activities — to children who might not experience them otherwise.

Gutheil, a member of the first group in the country to be trained in discipline-based arts education, recalled her fears that she would be unable to apply what she had learned at the first Florida Institute for Art Education (where she and Roucher originally met) to her classroom teaching. Most of the material presented there had been geared to elementary school children — older than those with whom Gutheil works. Furthermore, her students — from marginal socioeconomic groups — were part of a transient population and had limited language skills when they entered school. "It was rare," Gutheil recounted, "for them to know colors and shapes, or even how to count." However, by making art the core of her curriculum, Gutheil found she could easily teach them many concepts, from "in and out" to mathematical ideas. As the year progressed, the children's language skills and vocabulary expanded. They displayed new attention to detail, engaged in more sophisticated problem solving, were more thoughtful about their activities, and tried to express on paper the ideas derived from their experiences with art.

Not only did they gain knowledge of artists and art history, but their personal connections with art further engaged them in the learning process. One of her students fell in love with the *Mona Lisa*, because, as Gutheil quoted her, "My mama smiles like *Mona Lisa*." The children's artwork was also very expressive, providing amazing examples of the learning process that had been developing within them.

Roucher noted that when the Florida Institute began, the print collection used in the classrooms consisted primarily of Eurocentric art. Though the availability of non-Western images has increased, at that time, Gutheil had to rely primarily on what was on hand in creating her own lessons and approach. One participant observed that Gutheil's experience illustrated that teachers cannot always wait until they have all the materials they need. If teachers do not start because they lack a full range of appropriate materials, children will lose ground. Others found Gutheil to be, as one said, "a good example of what the classroom teacher, who has contact with the children all day long, can do."

Arts Education as a Catalyst to Reform:
Cultural Diversity

Speakers:

F. Graeme Chalmers, *Professor of Art Education, Department of Visual and Performing Arts in Education, University of British Columbia*
Judith M. Bryant, *Art Specialist and Consultant to the Multicultural/Multiethnic Education Office, Portland (Oregon) Public Schools*

Despite the gap between Canadian and American arts education expenditures ($1.40 per child in Canada versus $0.15 in the United States), Graeme Chalmers informed the audience that Canadians are also undergoing agonizing self-scrutiny about whether the arts are being adequately served in education. Turning to the importance of multicultural education, Chalmers noted that in the United States by the year 2000, 34 percent of children under eighteen will be African American, Latino, Asian American, or another minority. By the year 2010, minority children will comprise the majority of the population in the chief provinces. Yet, minority teachers will decrease from one in eight to one in twenty. These figures underscore the importance of a diverse education in preparing students to live in a pluralistic, multicultural society.

"A multicultural approach presumes that the arts have a significant role in human life and are present in all cultures." For new approaches to teaching the arts, Chalmers pointed to three recent studies of the social and personal functions of art, by Ellen Dissanayake, Louis Lankford, and June McFee. Dissanayake explores the therapeutic capacity of the arts in providing meaning and intensity to human life, while Lankford analyzes their economic worth, emotional impact, social and political power, as well as their ability to inspire and inform. McFee argues that the arts make values and emotions tangible, transmit and generate meaning, stabilize cultures, and perpetuate notions of reality.

These analyses can inform the curriculum. Students can examine how the visual arts, music, dance, and theater objectify and perpetuate cultural values. Young people's social consciousness and interpersonal communication are also affected by the arts, which provide unique avenues for self-expression. "Good arts programs will give students the opportunity to develop and delight in technical accomplishment."

Far from discarding the Western canon, Chalmers argued that we need to "'anthropologize' the West, to demonstrate how exotic its reality has become and how its claims to truth are linked to social practice." And while teachers cannot be fully conversant in every culture's art forms, he insisted that they must know enough to become facilitators, rather than transmitters, of knowledge. Chalmers strongly believes that the goal of arts education in a multicultural society is creating "an understanding of the important role played by the arts in all human activity. Participation in the arts must not be regarded as trivial; it needs to be seen as a central activity that gives a purpose to life."

Judith Bryant agreed that art is the ideal vehicle for preparing students to adjust to a diverse and changing world. One of Portland's Art Framework goals is that "instruction should not tell students what art is. Rather, it should provide a more inclusive picture and give students a framework to decipher and determine for themselves the meaning and value of art." The Multicultural/Multiethnic Education Office and the Portland Public School Board are finding ways to attain the goal of cross-cultural education through all disciplines, including the arts. Baseline essays are currently being developed on African Americans, Native Americans, Asian Americans, European Americans, Latin Americans, and Pacific Island Americans, to provide teachers with the basic information necessary to instruct students in each of the groups' history and culture.

One of the most important demands of the Portland Art Curriculum is that curricula include images by artists from a variety of ethnicities and cultures, as well as those by women. Although it has been difficult to find textbooks that "deal with more than one issue at a time," Bryant warned textbook representatives that "if you do not produce what we need, we are not going to buy the materials. We will not let textbooks drive our curriculum." Bryant proposed four key areas of concentration that schools, teachers, arts administrators, and art educators should focus on during this time of education reform: advocacy, teacher training, curriculum, and community.

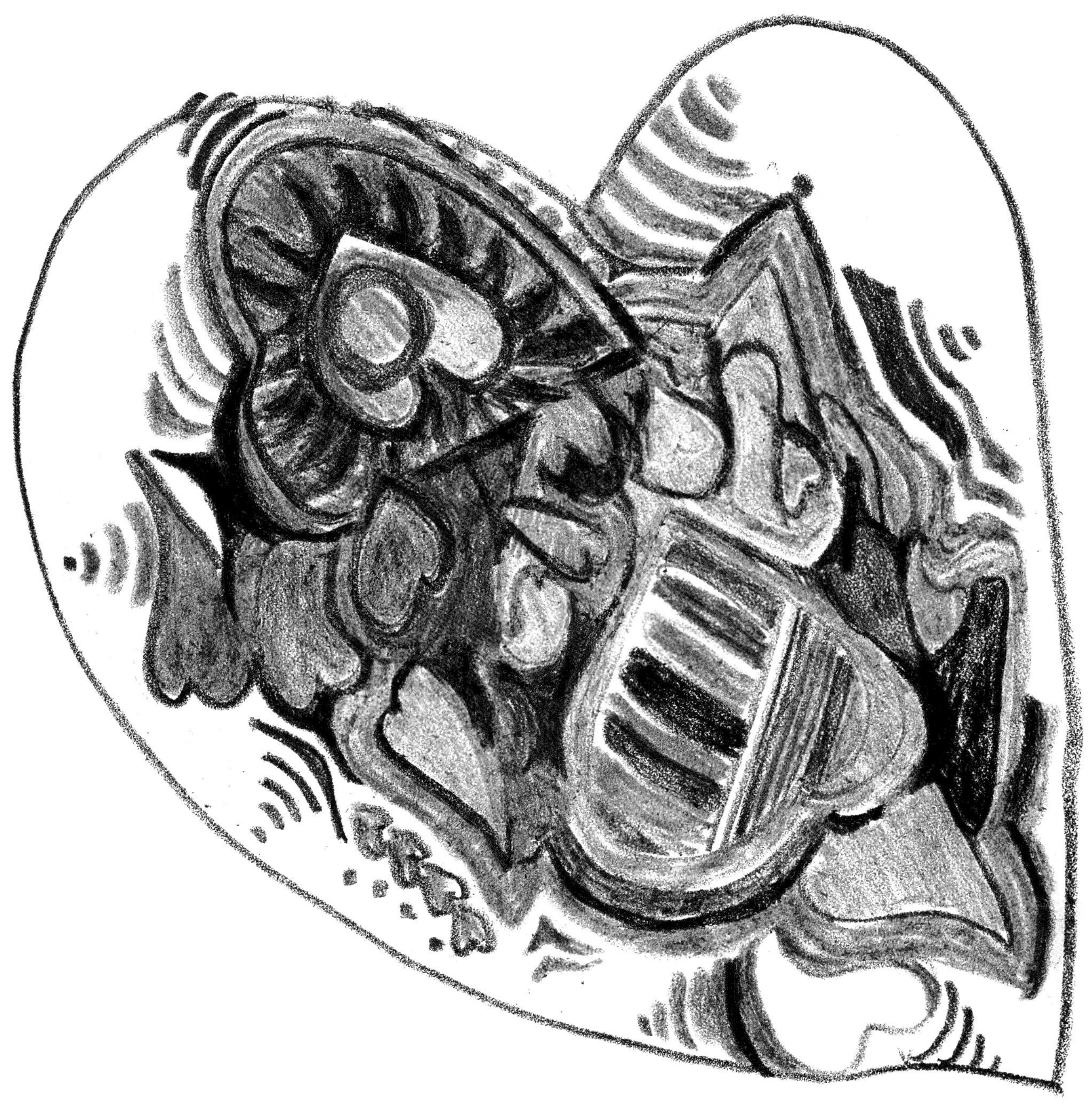

Arts Education as a Catalyst to Reform: Technology

Speakers:

LAURA A. LONDON, *Manager, K-12 Education Programs, Autodesk, Inc.*

HAL JOSEPHSON, *Director of Industry Relations, The 3DO Company*

Introducer:

JAMES A. MECKLENBURGER, *President, The Mecklenburger Group*

Many educators see technology as being at odds with their basic task and assume that "a choice must be made between technology and humanity." LAURA LONDON reported that Autodesk, Inc., aims to "close the gap between humanity and technology" by providing high-quality educational computer tools that facilitate very human processes. Several of Autodesk's software programs invite students to explore their own creativity by opening new avenues of expression.

London introduced a multimedia project using Autodesk software that the company conducted in collaboration with three middle schools in the Novato (California) Unified School District. Project organizers asked students, through the use of Autodesk software, to become city planners. The students imagined themselves traveling through a city in a bubble and visualized the city from various points of view. They envisioned themselves as architects, musicians, and astronauts to consider the city from above, below, and along the horizon. Subsequently, they recorded their impressions of how those different angles changed their perspective and then shared their thoughts in group discussions. These new virtual points of view prepared students for the project's second stage.

The students were divided into three groups and were introduced to two Autodesk computer programs: 3D Studio® and Autodesk Cyberspace Developer Kit (virtual reality), which allowed them to create geometric forms and add light, colors, and shadows. The first group was asked to build their own virtual city. These students developed a three-dimensional model of "Shape City" by assigning colors and materials to the forms that defined the land and cityscapes. The second group represented the computer *itself* in a virtual-reality collage. The third group designed a three-dimensional model of the "difference between school and education." All three groups dealt with sophisticated issues of scale, perspective, and geometric form, while exercising artistic creativity, working collaboratively, and solving technical and aesthetic problems.

Throughout the project, students kept journals of their virtual experiences and discussed the design process with students in the other groups. They reported being quite happy with their respective projects. The computer technology motivated them and riveted their interest. They especially enjoyed taking responsibility for their choices because it left them with a feeling that their opinions and decisions *mattered*.

One of the school principals involved in the project, Michael Watenpaugh, saw in those students involved improved communications skills, changed approaches to thinking, and expanded perspective. He declared that the project "only scratched the surface of the exciting and creative opportunities emerging through collaborations between business and arts education" and illustrated Gordon Ambach's observation that "the arts are the key to a sense of what is not yet."

HAL JOSEPHSON announced that 3DO planned to unveil the Panasonic-manufactured unit that will revolutionize interactive multimedia. The hardware uses the proprietary 3DO chips, which consist of a high-powered graphics animation engine that sprays sixty million pixels per second, ten times the equivalent digital pixels generated by a video signal in a home television set. The units will also play compact audio discs and will be compatible with Kodak's new photographic compact disc technology. Josephson concluded his presentation with a software demonstration that showed the power and capabilities of this new interactive technology and offered a glimpse of the future possibilities.

Arts Education Partnership Working Group

Speaker:

JAMES D. WOLFENSOHN, *Chairman, Board of Trustees, John F. Kennedy Center for the Performing Arts; Chairman, Arts Education Partnership Working Group*

Introducer:

HAROLD M. WILLIAMS, *President and Chief Executive Officer, J. Paul Getty Trust; Vice Chair, Arts Education Partnership Working Group*

Visual literacy has become a prerequisite to being an educated person, claimed HAROLD WILLIAMS. Young people must now be able to understand the historical and cultural context of our culture's overwhelming profusion of images and make sound aesthetic and moral judgments about them. "If we do not teach our students to do this by integrating the arts in the most basic way into school curricula," he warned, "we will fail our future citizens and, eventually, the cause of democracy." Despite obstacles to the integration of the arts into the curriculum, Williams believes that opportunities for arts education have never been greater. Even the press is displaying a fresh view of the importance of arts education.

JAMES WOLFENSOHN recalled that he initially came to the Kennedy Center to reposition the institution as a strong, viable center for the nation's performing arts. At that time, ironically, it was the only institution of its scale operating in the nation's capitol without federal dollars. Wolfensohn's difficulty in obtaining financial support from Congress led him to realize that a strong lobbying force is required to communicate that "the arts are not an optional extra, but are essential to the lives of our children."

After the National Education Goals were formulated, Wolfensohn initiated discussions with then Secretary of Education Lamar Alexander that led to the March 1991 America 2000 Arts Partnership statement. This document affirmed the importance of the arts in education and the need to develop "world-class standards" for learning in the arts. The Arts Partnership document also proposed a national center for arts education, an expansion of the National Assessment of Educational Progress (NAEP) to include the arts, the development of a research agenda in arts education, and the design of a national arts education dissemination network.

Wolfensohn chaired the Arts Education Partnership Working Group, which planned to submit its recommendations to the new administration. These recommendations include a plan to operate the national center for arts education as a national clearinghouse for the wealth of experience and information on arts education that already exists and provide ready access to that information through computers, videos, print materials, and other media. The Arts Education Partnership Working Group hopes the new administration will expand the initiative to include information about education in mathematics, science, history, and other subjects, and to create a common base of knowledge about "how history [for example] can be taught through art, how a local performing arts center is working with a school district, or how to get performing artists into the schools." The group also reviewed and recommended professional developments in teacher education.

The critical importance of partnerships among schools, museums, and performing arts organizations should not be underestimated, Wolfensohn emphasized. These linkages have enormous potential for improving the quality of arts education and stimulating the creativity of all the nation's citizens.

Art Education's Value in Interdisciplinary Learning

Speaker:
J. CARTER BROWN, *Director Emeritus, National Gallery of Art*
Respondent:
LYNETTE RINEHART, *Former Principal, Aiken Elementary School, Consolidated School District of Aiken County (South Carolina)*
Introducer:
BONNIE P. PITMAN, *Deputy Director, University Art Museum and Pacific Film Archive, University of California, Berkeley*

In introducing J. Carter Brown, BONNIE PITMAN noted that he is one of the nation's most important arts advocates and a vocal supporter for using the country's museums as teaching tools. The National Gallery of Art has implemented some of the most prominent museum program resources for interdisciplinary learning, including teacher education programs, print materials, and videodiscs.

Lynette Rinehart is also an innovator, Bonnie Pitman noted, whose school has become a model for interdisciplinary learning. She has, for example, installed computers and a satellite dish in her school and established a music in education and technology program and an in-house television program.

J. CARTER BROWN attributed the nation's resistance to including the arts in the curriculum to a number of factors, including the shortness of the American school day, a Puritan legacy that identifies the arts with "the work of the devil," school boards and parents who seek to train rather than educate, discipline problems, and "the inertia of the status quo." However, he cited the current administration's acknowledgment of the value of the arts in education and the Advertising Council's commitment to create $30 million worth of national advertising for the arts and humanities for the National Cultural Alliance as signs of major improvement.

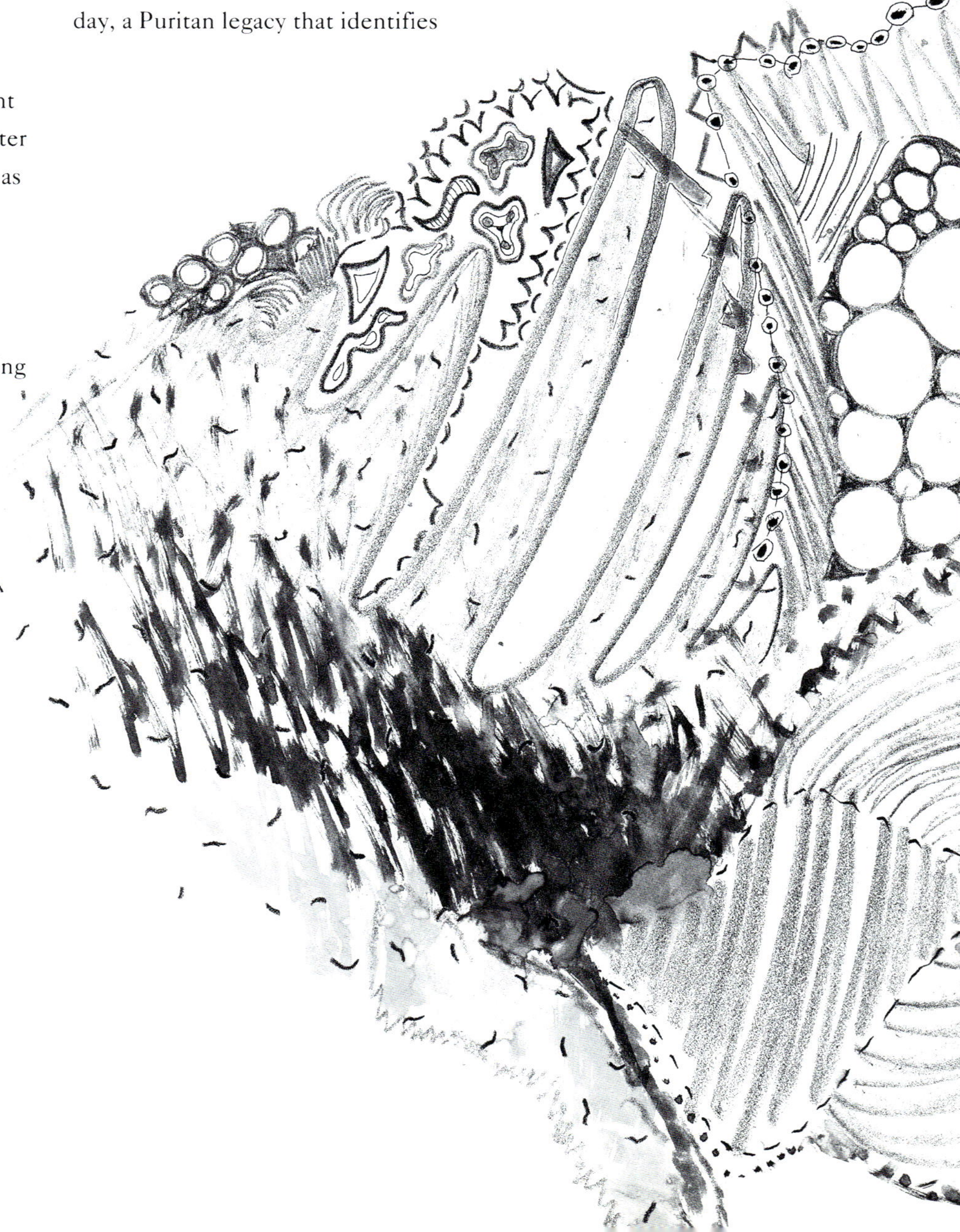

The education of the next generation must address "the whole child." Children should be educated to act creatively and responsibly in a multicultural world. Brown noted that the Smithsonian Institution is launching a three-year integrated curriculum development project that will be a catalyst to "figure out how we learn."

Discipline-based art education can best be achieved by "teaching the teachers." Likewise the National Gallery has been moving in that direction by holding seminars on its collections and on art history for administrators and teachers in varied disciplines. Brown also announced the availability of a new laserdisc containing newly digitized images of some 2,600 works of American art, made possible by a grant from the Annenberg Foundation. Brown presented slides featuring artworks to illustrate the way the arts provide a foundation for learning in many subjects. Andrea del Castagno's *The Youthful David* can be a springboard for a study of the Bible, Italian Renaissance public culture, and Renaissance philosophy. El Greco's *Laocoön* can lead students to the work's literary source in Virgil's *Aeneid* and to the study of seventeenth-century Toledo and the Spanish Inquisition.

LYNETTE RINEHART reinforced Brown's argument for bringing the arts to the center of the education process. She called for breaking down barriers between disciplines and recognizing the need for teacher training in interdisciplinary education and urged the audience to capitalize on the growing consensus in favor of interdisciplinary learning. Her experience demonstrates that the arts help students to think and express themselves, making them active participants in the learning process. The arts nurture self-respect and self-esteem, enhance ethnic and cultural sensitivity, and humanize the learning environment. "They permeate every element of our existence."

Rinehart pointed out how advances in telecommunications further this process by linking students from all over the country — via computers and modems — to such educational resources as the National Gallery of Art and the Library of Congress. Noting that in the past four years her Aiken Elementary School pupils have consistently ranked between the 96th and the 99th percentiles among South Carolina schools, Rinehart concluded by saying, "You can see that arts education does a good job of connecting students not only with their past, but with their future as well."

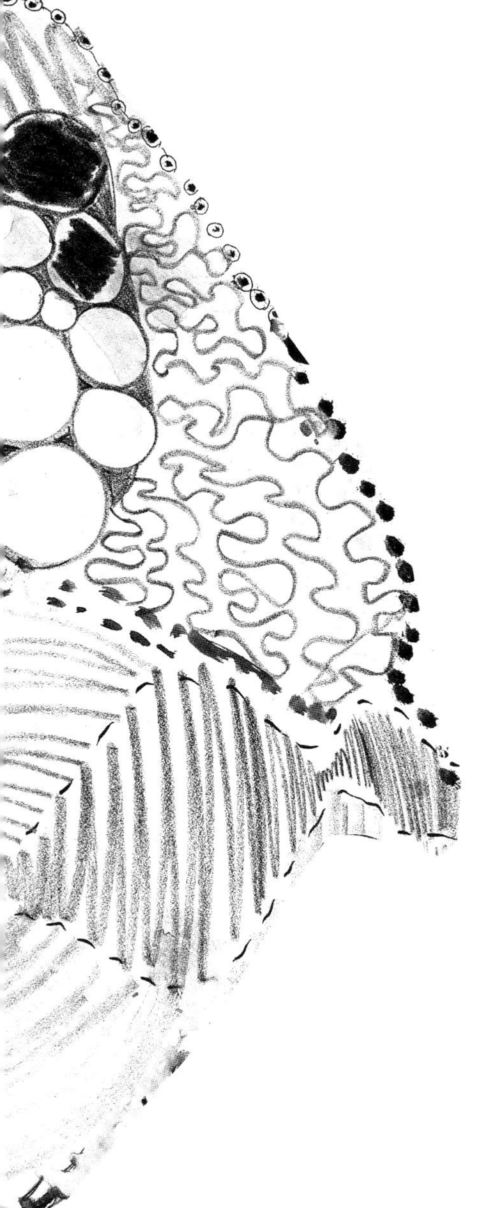

Speakers:

RUTH MITCHELL, *Associate
Director, Council for Basic
Education*

DENNIS PALMER WOLF, *Director,
Performance Assessment Collabora-
tives for Education; Senior Research
Associate, Graduate School of
Education, Harvard University*

Moderator:

EVA L. BAKER, *Professor of
Educational Psychology and Social
Research Methods, Graduate School
of Education, and Director, Center
for Evaluation, University of
California at Los Angeles;
Codirector, Center for Research on
Evaluation, Standards, and Student
Testing*

Introducer:

LEANNA LANDSMANN, *Publisher
and Consultant, Leanna
Landsmann, Inc.*

Assessment is a key focus of the
education reform policy debate. In
the classrooms LEANNA LANDSMANN
has visited, elementary teachers are
experimenting with portfolio
assessment, and students' learning
is being measured through projects
and performances — methods that
may be new to classroom teachers,
but are "old hat for arts educators."
Because of their experience with
alternative assessment techniques,
arts educators have an obligation to
play a leadership role in the national debate surrounding the reform of
assessment practices.

EVA BAKER discussed research
conducted by the Center for
Research on Evaluation Standards
and Student Testing on the effectiveness of performance-based
assessment and ways it can be
made more useful. She noted that
the primary reason for assessment
is to help students achieve and perform, as well as to report to funders
on the results of their support and
to gauge the indirect impact of arts
programs on students. Arts educators are also embracing assessment
for survival purposes.

Yet, there is little empirical
foundation for how assessments are
used in a large-scale context. Baker
emphasized that their validity lies
not in statistical coefficients but in
fairness and sensitivity to instructional differences and to their
effects on the system of education.
Thus far, assessments have not had
a positive impact on our system. If
assessment is to improve student
performance, it must be coupled
with corresponding support for arts
education.

RUTH MITCHELL agreed that
"the arts need assessment for their
survival." The link between assessment and education reform began
in the early 1980s with calls for
greater accountability and the
recognition that in portfolio and
performance assessments, the arts
had developed the most viable
alternatives to norm-referenced,
multiple-choice tests. Assessments
adapted from the arts provide many
of the practices envisioned by education reform and provide new
models for learning and instruction.
Music teachers in the Pittsburgh
Public Schools' ARTS PROPEL program have found that a portfolio-
based curriculum enables students
to become perceptive critics of
their own and colleagues' performances and thus to perform at
higher levels. Teachers have
reported that participating in the
design, development, administration, and scoring of performance
assessments is the best professional
development they have ever had.
The difficulties inherent in the
process have prompted a professional conversation among arts
teachers about values, standards,
and ways to reach them that has
never taken place before.

Attention will be drawn to the
arts by large-scale public assessment and the inclusion of the arts
in graduation requirements.
"Assessing the arts is another way
of saying that the arts are essential
in the education of every child."
Mitchell exhorted teachers to "look
beyond museums and concert halls.
Confront the art that bombards

Americans twenty-four hours a day" and help students effectively critique media-delivered art. Arts education must extend beyond the classroom, and television can be an ally in that effort.

DENNIS PALMER WOLF believes that "no amount of assessment matters if the curriculum is not worth assessing." Assessment allows educators to identify ideas they care about deeply and consider what it would mean for students to spend several years in pursuit of them. She described a classroom project in which teachers created performance assessments based on a work by African-American artist Faith Ringgold. Using diverse materials, students created work inspired by Ringgold's use of imagery, local color, detail, language, and metaphors. Scoring was based on criteria such as grounded imagination, inventions, and connections. Wolf urged teachers not to be propelled by the current anxiety about education reform into a wholesale emulation of mathematics and geography, but to remember "the complexity, imagination, depth, and variation that are intrinsic to the arts." In this context, Wolf urged arts educators to use performance assessments primarily for instructional purposes: for debating and teaching the criteria for strong and diverse work.

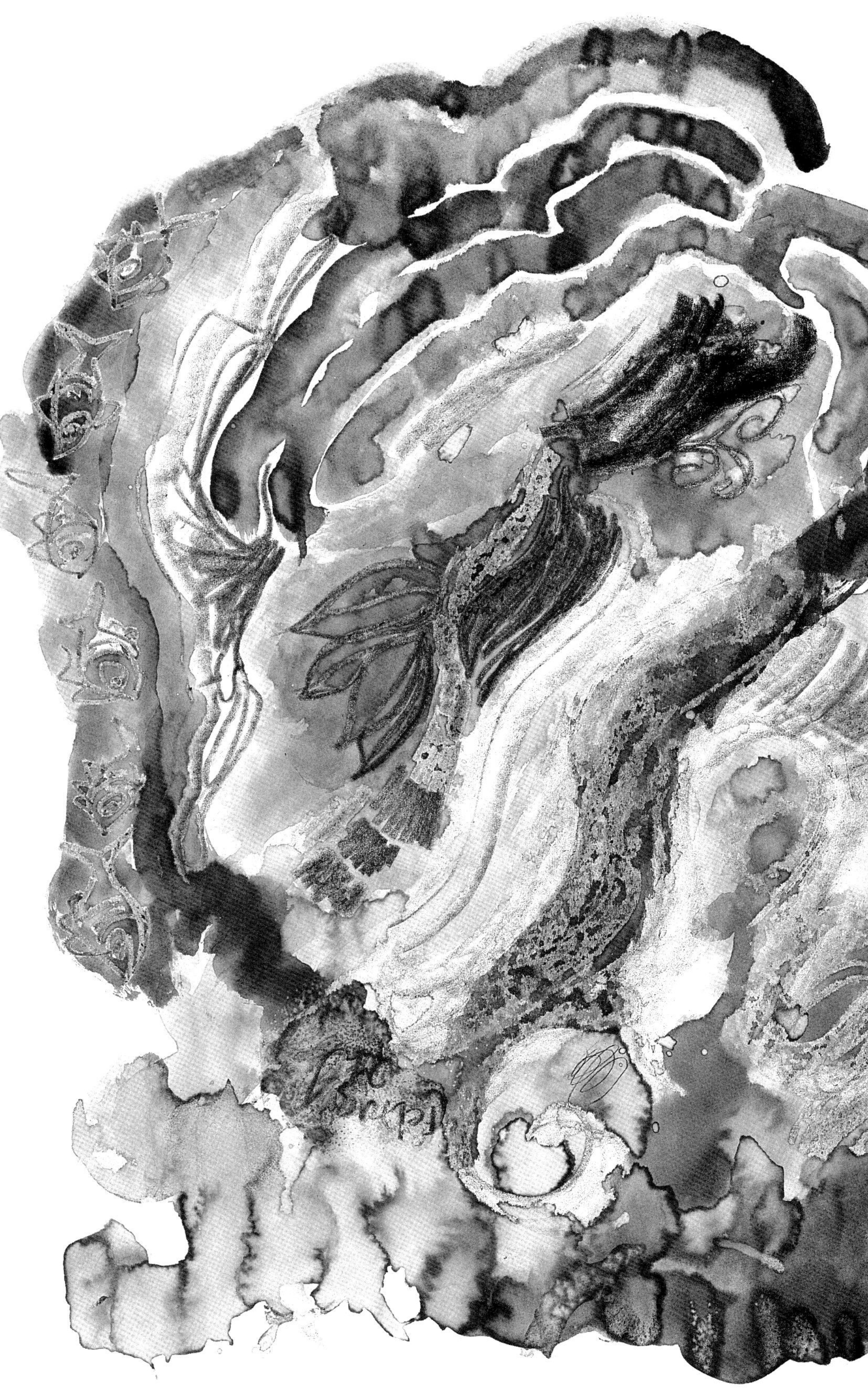

Understanding Cultural Diversity through Arts Education

Speaker:

VADA E. BUTCHER, *Dean Emerita, School of Fine Arts, Howard University*

Introducer:

MARTIN ROSENBERG, *Associate Professor of Art History, University of Nebraska*

VADA BUTCHER reviewed the history of cultural diversity in terms of its global manifestations, its role in the evolution of our national history, and its impact on public education. Three cultural streams — Native American, European, and African — converged to create American culture. These influences were joined later by Latin-American and Asian cultural forces. Despite the country's ideals, European cultural norms have dominated for over 500 years. This hegemony is now being challenged not only by ethnic minorities, but by previously ignored sectors of the population, such as women, the physically disabled, and lesbians and gays. To prepare students to live comfortably and productively with people who have different worldviews, our education system must accommodate the increasing diversity of our society. Curricula must not only reflect other cultures, but involve "different ways of knowing."

Concerns that diversity will dilute the curriculum or preclude all but the most superficial study can be addressed by carefully structuring syllabi, goals, and objectives. "Equity need not preclude excellence," Butcher remarked. Arts education courses must reflect the complexity of the nation's cultural diversity and provide experiences that enhance understanding of art as the expression of a given culture. Students must be able to apply appropriate criteria in evaluating the productions of various cultures.

The arts also provide insight into the psychological trauma suffered by minority groups in their attempts to adopt the dominant culture's worldview. Butcher reviewed African-American religious music and literature for examples of what W. E. B. DuBois called the "double consciousness" minorities acquire, that is the sense of always looking at oneself through the eyes of others. These ranged from the spirituals of enslaved African Americans to works by composer William Grant.

"Only the arts can reveal the spirit and soul of a nation committed to social equity, celebrate its triumphs and mourn its failures in the pursuit of that ideal, and interpret its dreams for the unity of its peoples in the future."

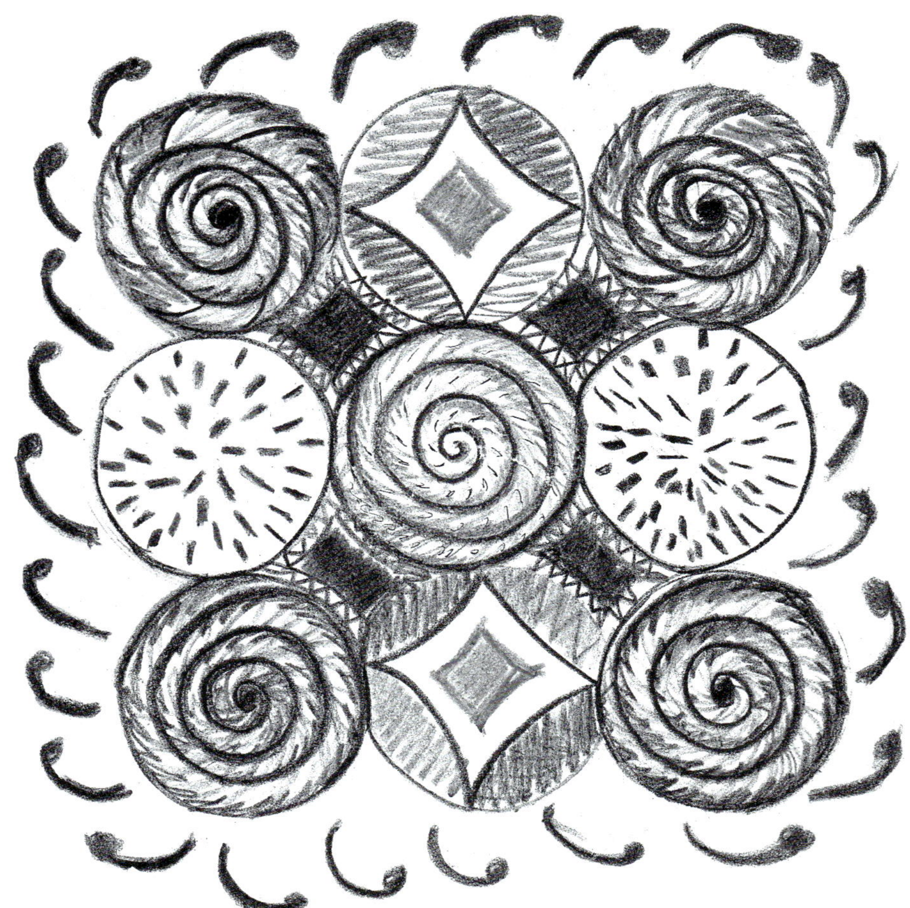

Equity and Access through Arts Education

Speaker:

MICHAEL GREENE, *President and Chief Executive Officer, National Association of Recording Arts and Sciences, Inc.*

Introducer:

JUDITH M. BRYANT, *Art Specialist and Consultant to the Multicultural/Multiethnic Office Portland (Oregon) Public Schools*

MICHAEL GREENE is convinced that the scenario of "back-to-basics conservatives who pray to the gods of Eurocentricity to deliver us from the evils of the dark, freethinking radicals hell-bent on trashing our canons and rulebooks to make room for multiculturalism and self-expression" presents a false dichotomy. An inclusive education agenda that sacrifices neither discipline nor individual expression is needed to redeploy our educational and cultural resources in a way that ensures our cultural survival.

Across America, schoolchildren are deprived of opportunities to learn about their rich and varied musical heritage — "casualties in a war of narrow minds and misappropriated resources." This did not happen over a short period of time, but is the product of an erosion of American cultural values. Nor can the problem be redressed in two or three years.

However, from South Carolina to the South Bronx, schools have been revitalized by arts programs. And experience shows that when the arts are emphasized, attendance improves, as do math and reading scores. The Academy of Recording Arts and Sciences is calling attention to the musical arts and the importance of music and arts education. The Academy is doing its part to improve America's arts environment through programs such as the Grammys in the Schools, the Grammy All-American High School Band, and the attention the Grammy Awards give the arts in "the very hot, bright spotlight" of its annual awards ceremony, which attracts the world's largest television audience.

Yet, while Japan annually spends $4.80 per pupil on arts education, Germany spends $2.40, Austria and Sweden spend $2.00, Canada $1.40, and the United Kingdom $1.20, the United States spends a mere $0.15. Only a quarter of California's 420 elementary schools offer music, and only 4 percent of students are directly involved in music education.

Plato considered music to be the most potent of the arts because it reaches to the soul and imparts grace. Confucius believed that only men who studied music were fit to govern. "We have obviously gone downhill since then," Greene declared. If conventional wisdom prevails and the arts are no longer considered basic to a high-quality education, they will become "an elite privilege for the enrichment of the few; no longer a source of self-discovery, but of cultural alienation." This is not the time "to raise the cultural drawbridge" and close our ears to rappers and metalheads or any other forms of musical expression unfamiliar to us. Rather, it is a time to explore, to experience. He insisted, "It takes no more energy to aspire to the highest standards than it does to locate the lowest common denominator."

Conference Summation

Speakers:

JAMES G. BERK, *Executive Director, National Academy of Recording Arts and Sciences Foundation, Inc.; Former Principal, the Hamilton High Schools Complex, Los Angeles*

PAULA EVANS, *Director, National Re:Learning Faculty, Coalition of Essential Schools, Brown University*

ELLIOT W. EISNER, *Professor of Education and Art, Stanford University*

Introducer:

LEILANI LATTIN DUKE, *Director, Getty Center for Education in the Arts*

Before addressing the restructuring of America's schools for the twenty-first century, JAMES BERK registered dismay over the negative attitudes expressed in the video-taped focus group conversation, *"Why Are the Arts Essential to Education Reform?"* Especially disturbing were perceptions that teachers do not want to change and that an elitist arts community is the key barrier to arts education. The discussion gave Berk a clearer understanding of the challenges facing arts educators in overcoming popular misconceptions.

Educators clearly want twenty-first-century citizens to be well-versed in technology and to be proficient communicators and critical thinkers who function easily in a multilingual, multicultural world. From the standpoint of access and equity, however, "we know we are failing. The traditional agrarian, White, middle-class system of education is unable to respond to the current cultural and economic diversity." Berk regards the blame-oriented attitude — on the part of students, parents, administrators, school boards, and state and federal government — as the source of the problem. Educators must form a cohesive, unified coalition and become more proactive to effect positive change.

Berk reviewed strategies for change that had been proposed during the conference, including installation of high school master programs and the institution of graduation requirements in the arts. The best way to get such proposals implemented is to lobby state school boards, "the people who dictate what happens in the states." He also urged educators to form partnerships with businesses, like the National Academy of Recording Arts and Sciences Foundation's joint venture with the Los Angeles Community Redevelopment Agency, a school district, a high school, the Music Performance Trust Fund, and a musicians' union. This program has arranged interactive concerts for over 5,000 children.

PAULA EVANS described her work at the National Re:Learning Faculty Project of the Coalition of Essential Schools, a national secondary-school reform effort involving approximately 450 schools. She noted the persuasive cases made at the conference for including the arts in the curriculum, using technology to "invent tomorrow's schools," implementing new assessment forms, and constructing interdisciplinary curricula.

However, Evans hoped participants would not become too distracted because the arts were not initially included in the National Education Goals. She pointed out that "few teachers on the local level even know those goals exist." Changing the perception of education will be an uphill battle because many classrooms still resemble those used by earlier generations and most city schools are dysfunctional after years of neglect.

"Even the arts will fail in the current school setting because the structure of our schools does not nurture the human spirit." New technologies, interdisciplinary curricula, and new assessment methods cannot simply be imposed on the existing system. "The arts community must work with its colleagues across the disciplines to restructure schools, fostering those qualities that best embody what teaching and learning is all about."

ELLIOT EISNER observed that implementation of the interdisciplinary approach advocated during the conference will require major changes in schools' organizational structure and in teacher education. To foster the values that most educators and artists espouse, offer intellectual and creative stimulation, and amplify intercultural understanding, schools must also be "recultured." Those in the classroom must not only be retrained, they must understand that the arts offer "a way of thinking about thinking," and that "with art, one solves problems, while with math, one performs tasks." Because the thinking generated by the arts plays a central role in sophisticated cognition, the arts represent an education model for other subjects to emulate.

Eisner also pointed to the problematic character of standards in determining instructional effectiveness, noting that the term is used rather glibly despite the fact that its meaning is unclear. "We cannot afford to be unanalytical about such a key concept if we are going to engage in significant education reform."

Eisner added his support to the call for the arts to be required for high school and college graduation. He concluded that, in school improvement, "we need to think not only about the children, but also about the adults who work in the schools, because the schools will not be any better for the children than they are for the teachers and administrators who work there."

Unity through the Arts

Speakers:
BEN VEREEN, *Entertainer*
LEILANI LATTIN DUKE, *Director,
Getty Center for Education in
the Arts*
Introducer:
PAT HENRY, *President, The
National Parent Teacher
Association*

This session began with the video *Say Yes to Life*. Its subject is an innovative, interdisciplinary initiative at the Hamilton Middle School (Long Beach, California), undertaken to combat the loss of self-esteem that was a by-product of attending Chapter I remedial classes. The students and teachers produced a music video featuring a rap song that urged other children to "go to school, get an education, so we can have a much better generation."

PAT HENRY explained that what she learned in her early years with the local PTA was "what I want to do for my child, I must first do for all children." She encouraged all parents to become involved with their local PTAs because "every education report documents that students do better when parents are involved." She stressed the importance of arts education to the growth of our children— emotionally, academically, and culturally.

BEN VEREEN'S interest in the arts began in Brooklyn during his childhood with the respite that dance lessons provided from community violence. Dance led Vereen out of the ghetto and, he says, "was the vehicle that motivated me to commit myself to the arts and education."

Vereen pointed out that, in considering the importance of science and the arts, one should remember that the arts came first. Even Alexander Graham Bell's great invention, the telephone, was a product of creativity. As a form of communication, art helps people share their cultures. When introduced to children at an early age, art motivates them to learn.

Vereen urged participants to spread the word that the arts community is not divided, but united. An example is the Chicago Awareness Group, which is made up of artists and entertainers who have joined with business, foundation, community, and arts education leaders to provide information on a wide variety of arts education programs through a toll-free number. Recalling the Chinese proverb, "It is better to light a candle than curse the darkness," Vereen hoped participants would keep the candle lit.

LEILANI LATTIN DUKE thanked participants for contributing to an invigorating exchange of information and views. As they returned to their daily lives, she hoped they would keep the spirit of the conference alive and increase support for the arts in education. She asked that each pledge to convert one other person to the cause of the arts in education and "go out there with the message, 'The arts, stupid.'"

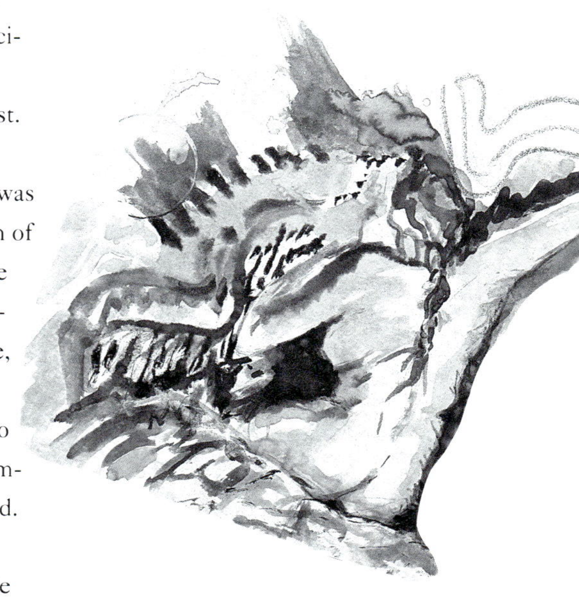

Postconference Session:

Discussion of the Recommendations of the Arts Education Partnership Working Group

Speaker:

DAVID O'FALLON, *Staff Director, Arts Education Partnership Working Group*

Introducer:

HAROLD M. WILLIAMS, *President and Chief Executive Officer, J. Paul Getty Trust; Vice Chair, Arts Education Partnership Working Group*

HAROLD WILLIAMS identified four basic aspects of arts education: to create and perform the arts; to understand the arts' importance in culture and history; to perceive and respond to the inherent qualities of the arts; and to make sound judgments with an understanding of the bases on which these judgments rest.

DAVID O'FALLON pointed out that the title of the conference, "Achieving National Education Reform: Arts Education as Catalyst," suggested the power of the arts to transform education. He was convinced that a national center for arts education is a critical

step in fulfilling this potential by making what the arts education community has already learned immediately accessible and widely available. The center would be a coordinating, facilitating network rather than a "top-down-driven we'll-tell-you-what's-best organization." More than a database, it would identify strategies and practices that have worked — information currently only in the minds of teachers, artists-in-residence, and administrators. The center would not be a funding source but a bridge between the worlds of art and education. Neither a library nor a repository, it would actively compile and distribute information and encompass a wide range of communications technology, including print, videos, and compact discs.

O'Fallon recommended that the initial steps to form the center begin in the next year. At the very least, the creation of an electronic network would allow those in the field to communicate. With a grant from the National Endowment for the Arts, the planning phase has already been completed. A national center would need the support of the Department of Education and the National Endowment for the Arts. A pilot program including the establishment of a national center and involving two or three pilot networks would cost $500,000, and a full national center could be modestly operated for $1,000,000 a year. O'Fallon devised these estimates with the aim of leaving no one out of the network because of cost: "It is in the essential nature of this work that it should be democratic."

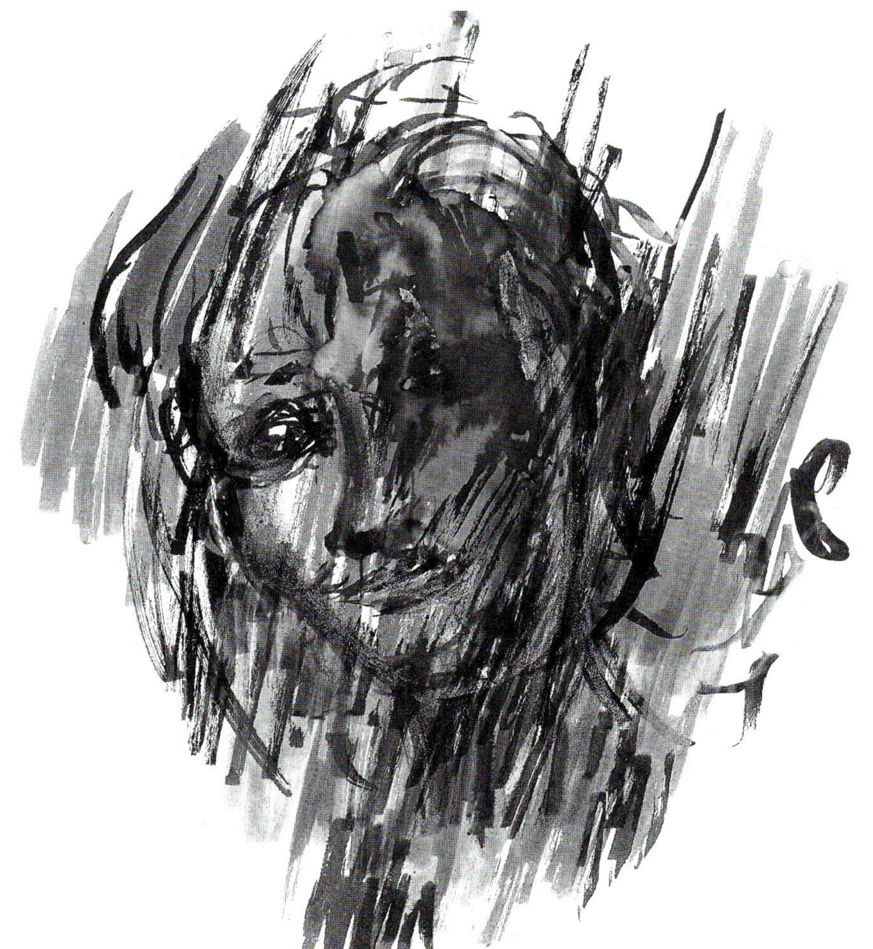

Acknowledgments

THE J. PAUL GETTY TRUST

HAROLD M. WILLIAMS
President and Chief Executive
Officer

LEILANI LATTIN DUKE
Director
Getty Center for Education in the Arts

ANN BASSI
Program Officer
Getty Center for Education in the Arts

THANDIWEE MICHAEL KENDALL
Program Officer
Getty Center for Education in the Arts

ELIZABETH PAUL
Senior Program Associate
Getty Center for Education in the Arts

VICKI ROSENBERG
Program Officer
Getty Center for Education in the Arts

NATALIE STERBA
Administrative Manager
Getty Center for Education in the Arts

KATHY TALLEY-JONES
Managing Editor
Getty Center for Education in the Arts

ROBIN NELSON WICKS
Intern
Getty Center for Education in the Arts

JULIE ABEL
ROZITA AFAR
MADELEINE COULOMBE
MARY DAY
MICHAEL FERRERA
ADRIENNE LEE
Administrative Staff
Getty Center for Education in the Arts

PHILIPPA CALNAN
Director of Public Affairs
J. Paul Getty Trust

KATHY BARRETO
Public Affairs Associate
J. Paul Getty Trust

*CONFERENCE DESIGN,
MANAGEMENT, AND PRODUCTION*
PACIFIC VISIONS COMMUNICATIONS, INC.

Direction:
VALSIN A. MARMILLION
President

Coordination:
RACHEL ROSENTHAL
Account Supervisor

Assistant Coordination:
CHRISTOPHER DOYLE
Account Executive

Additional Coordination:
ALEXIS ANDERSON
LISA BEST
JIM KILROY
LISA NOBLE
JENNY SIEGENTHALER
Pacific Visions Communications, Inc.

Editorial Photography:
WILLIAM F. CLARK PHOTOGRAPHY

Graphic Design:
IKKANDA DESIGN GROUP, INC.

Art Direction:
RICHARD IKKANDA
DONNA BEILOCK
SUZETTE HEIMAN
MOLLY McCORD

Conference Reporting and
Summary:
KEENS COMPANY

Project Director:
WILLIAM KEENS

Project Managing Editor:
REYNOLDS CHILDRESS

Project Coordinators:
GREGORY ROBY
TRACY ROTHSCHILD

Project Associates:
OLIVE MOSIER
ELIZA REILLY
MARCIA WADE

The illustrations that appear
throughout this publication were
created by conference participants
who drew with Crayola® products
provided courtesy of Binney &
Smith, Inc., during the final conference session.

Ordering Information

New Advocacy Resources from the Getty Center for Education in the Arts

Additional copies of ***Perspectives on Education Reform: Arts Education as Catalyst*** are available — Six leaders in business, the arts, education, and politics share their insights about the value of arts education; also includes the summary proceedings of the Getty Center's national conference, "Achieving National Education Reform: Arts Education as Catalyst," February 4–6, in San Francisco.

1993, $5.00, ISBN 0-89236-296-0, 8 1/2 × 11 inches, 60 pages

The Art of Learning — This special edition of the Learning Channel's *Teacher TV* series takes audiences to five schools across the country that have created enriched learning environments by making the arts the cornerstone of innovation. The program, hosted by Taran Noah Smith, star of ABC's *Home Improvement*, was coproduced by the Learning Channel, the National Education Association, and the Getty Center for Education in the Arts.

1993, $15.00, 1/2-inch VHS format, 60 minutes

"Why Are the Arts Essential to Education Reform?" — This production paints a revealing picture of the attitudes and issues surrounding the central place of the arts in education. The video consists of a 16-minute excerpt from an address by Gordon Ambach, executive director of the Council of Chief State School Officers, and a national leader in education policy. In addition, a provocative exchange between parents, educators, and government and business professionals exposes commonly held attitudes toward and expectations for art education.

1993, $10.00, 1/2-inch VHS format, 47 minutes

To order these resources, complete and send the enclosed order form or contact the Getty Trust Publications Distribution Center:

Getty Trust Publications
Distribution Center E20X
P.O. Box 2112
Santa Monica, CA
90407-2112

Telephone:
800/223-3431
Weekdays between
9:00 a.m. and
5:00 p.m. (PST)
Fax: 310/453-7966

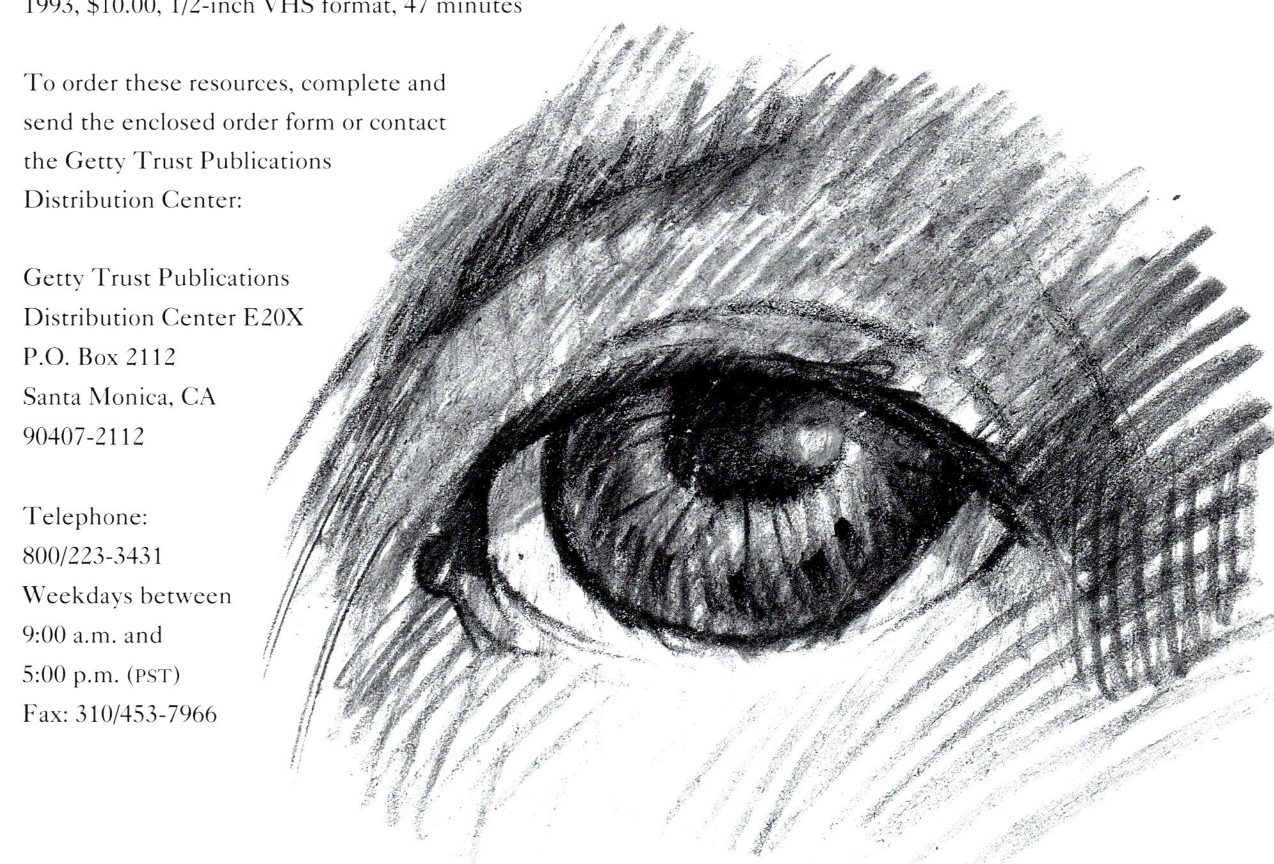